BAPTIZED INTO GOD'S FAMILY

The Doctrine of Infant Baptism for Today

Second Edition

A. Andrew Das

NORTHWESTERN PUBLISHING HOUSE
Milwaukee, Wisconsin

Second edition,   2008

Scripture taken from the
HOLY BIBLE, REVISED STANDARD VERSION

All rights reserved. No part of this publication may be
reproduced, stored in a retrieval system, or transmitted in
any form or by any means — electronic, mechanical, photo-
copying, recording, or otherwise — except for brief quota-
tions in reviews, without prior permission from the publisher.

Library of Congress Card 91-67125
Northwestern Publishing House
1250 N. 113th St., Milwaukee, WI 53226-3284
© 1991 by A. Andrew Das
Printed in the United States of America
ISBN 978-0-8100-0409-2

24 25 26 27 28 29 30 31 32 33   17 16 15 14 13 12 11 10 9 8

FOREWORD

I first met Andrew Das when I was preaching in a church in Houston. He was a little boy then. I next met him when he was my student in a class in the Lutheran Confessions. At that time I was amazed to learn that he as a college student had already written a book on baptism.

The book, enlarged and improved, I am sure, since then, is now being published by Northwestern Publishing House. It is truly a remarkable book. It is written on one of the most controverted and unappreciated articles of our Christian faith. Its audience is just about anybody at all—pastors, Christian lay people from any denomination, or interested readers who want to know what Christian baptism is all about and what the Scriptures say about it.

The book is winsome. Not only has Andrew Das written in a popular, understandable style, but he digs into the Scriptures in a way that every reader will perceive what God is saying about baptism. The book is also scholarly without being threatening. The author treats all the biblical material which deals with Christian baptism, and he thoroughly goes into the chief passages, even quoting (but also translating) a key Greek word at times.

Two very important comments must be made about this book, comments with which we wish to commend the book most highly. First, baptism is not treated as a minor ordinance or disconnected appendage to Christianity, but is related to the great biblical themes of sin and grace, faith and salvation. Second, baptism is shown to be not law, some ordinance, or work that I the Christian do, but a marvelous work of God's infinite grace for Christ's sake in me.

Andrew Das's little book will be a great blessing to anyone who reads it.

Dr. Robert D. Preus

CONTENTS

INTRODUCTION:
WHY BE CONCERNED ABOUT
INFANT BAPTISM?

Some two thousand years ago our Lord Jesus Christ gave to his church the gift of baptism. Scripture refers to this gift in many places. Yet what was given as a blessing seems at times to have become a curse. For the same two thousand years Christians have been unable to agree on the nature and meaning of this gift. Rather than binding together the family of God, baptism brought division and strife. Or so it seemed.

Indeed at one point, baptism seemed to become a curse for me as well. I was a Lutheran from birth. I was baptized as an infant. I believed in Jesus as my Savior as far back as I can remember (age three). Before I was confirmed, I was shown Scripture to help me see what God did in my baptism. It all made sense to me. I had *always* believed in Jesus, since my baptism.

As a college student I met a wonderful Christian girl. While her church background was not the same as my own, our relationship grew strong over the course of two years. Yet a single issue seemed to divide us. Her church did not believe in infant baptism. Nor did she. Nothing I said seemed to shake her conviction.

As young people do, we had talked about marriage. But what were we to do with the children? Baptize them as babies? Only if we baptized them again later on when they confessed their faith. But wait a minute! That didn't make much sense. It was a compromise. And a shoddy one at that! What should two Christian parents do? And why?

So we went back to the Scriptures. And from there, we went around and around. Surely two Bible-believing Christians should be able to reach an understanding! But we didn't. That doesn't take away from the Word of God. It just means that we sometimes get in the way of that Word.

In the process, infant baptism became for me a matter of law—*God's* law. We *have to* baptize babies. So I used Scripture like a sledgehammer. Perhaps you can relate to that. Christians have a way of using the Word like that all the time. Maybe it's just our sinful flesh. . . . (We'll have to come back to that one.) Only later did I come to see the error of my ways. Infant baptism was never meant to be pushed onto people. It was never an Eleventh Commandment. No, infant baptism was given to us as an expression of God's free *grace*. And that's how we have to think and speak of it!

Maybe that's why my college sweetheart and I never came to agree. When you try to motivate people by the law, you only arouse a rebellious spirit. No, we have to persuade one another gently, and in love. Surely, if infant baptism is an authentic blessing of God's grace, the Scriptures should bear that out.

As time went on, I found out that the objections my friend had were the same ones others had too. Isn't baptism only helpful if a person believes? And how does an infant "believe"? And where in the Bible does it ever say to baptize babies? Whoever said baptism saves, let alone that infants need that salvation in the same way as adults? Are infants really sinful? And couldn't God deal with infants in his own special way?

Do any of these questions sound familiar to you? I'm

sure some of them do. But how would one answer these questions? What Scripture would bear on the issues? As I searched for material to help me, I didn't find a single source that effectively dealt with the full gamut of issues that infant baptism brings up. That fact, along with experiences talking with other people, showed me that it was time to look at infant baptism afresh.

I invite you to come with me on a journey through the Scriptures as we see what God's will is for these little ones. Infants are important people too! They are just as important as any of us. Christians today are very concerned about the abortion issue. Not to diminish that issue, but people discussing abortion often are treating merely the physical side of life. How much greater are the stakes with infant baptism—the spiritual life of infants! God wants to provide babies a new life in Christ. He works his will for the infant by the baptism that the church administers in his stead.

Whether you agree with me or not, surely you would agree that the issues themselves are major ones. Consider if what I'm saying is true. If indeed the Bible *does* teach baptism as his means of saving the infant, we don't want to stand in the way of God's saving work! So at least join with me on this journey through the authoritative Word of God, the Scriptures.

Heavenly Father, we come before you today confessing our sinfulness. But you saved us from our sins by the saving work of the crucified Lord Jesus Christ. We didn't deserve to be saved; yet you have saved us. We praise you for that. But often our sins still get in the way of our hearing your Word. We pray that you open our hearts and minds, even as when you first opened our ears to salvation. Make us diligent and faithful to that Word in our lives. In your mercy we pray this through Jesus Christ, your Son, our Lord. Amen.

1.

BAPTISM AND ORIGINAL SIN

"He's got the dimples of his father."

"He's a cutie alright," responded Marcie. Janet was holding the quietly slumbering babe in her arms. She and her husband had wanted a baby for a number of years. Finally, little Michael came along.

"I can't get over how peaceful he looks when he's sleeping," said Janet.

"Janet, are you going to get the baby baptized?"

"Well, Marcie, we don't baptize babies in my church."

"Why not?"

Janet paused for a second as she shifted Michael over a bit. "We believe that baptism is for a new Christian. Once a person realizes his sinfulness, then he can get baptized. But a little baby can't sin like that."

Janet's answer took Marcie by surprise. She had never really thought about it that way before.

"You really don't think so?"

Janet smiled. "Marcie, have you ever heard of a baby murdering someone? Or a baby stealing? Michael's just a baby. He's totally unconscious about things like that. Just look at him sleeping here."

1

Janet had a hard time seeing the need for infant baptism. After all, if infants are too young to really sin, what's the need for baptism? Notice also how Janet saw sin in terms of the actual deeds that were done. But sin is much more than that! It's also a state, a condition that we are in . . . from the time of conception and birth.

The Scriptures on original sin

In other words, the story of baptism goes back to the very beginning. The story began with sin. God had created man and placed him in the Garden of Eden. Genesis 1:26,27 says: "Then God said, 'Let us make man in our image, after our likeness. . . .' So God created man in his own image, in the image of God he created him." After God created the world, Genesis 3 tells of the fall into sin. Genesis 3 paints a dark picture in contrast to the creation account. Man was ashamed of himself. He hid from God. The earth was cursed because of man's sin. Death became the inevitable.

This dark picture continues all through the early chapters of Genesis. The curse on Cain, the Flood, and Babel are all further results of sin, a tragic contrast to the dignity of man in the creation. As Genesis 6:5 says: "The Lord saw that the wickedness of man was great in the earth, and that every imagination of the thoughts of his heart was only evil continually."

In the midst of the bleak images from the Fall come the words of Genesis 5:3. Seth is born in *Adam's* image and likeness! Adam's sin had tainted the image of God in him. Seth inherited a tainted image of God. So Genesis 5 continues on with the lineage from Adam and Seth. Like a funeral dirge, the words "and he died" repeat themselves through the names of Adam's descendants. People were born only to die. Such are the natural results of sin. So Genesis 8:21 can say that man's thoughts are evil from his youth, from his childhood.

Indeed, people are evil from their very conception!

Job 14:1 states: "Man that is born of a woman is of a few days and it is full of trouble." But it's not just that man *does* evil from his conception. Man *is* evil from the womb. Job 14:4, a few verses later, adds: "Who can bring a clean thing out of an unclean? There is not one." Jesus affirms these words in Matthew 7:17 when he says that a corrupt tree can only bring forth corrupt fruit. Job 15:14 says: "What is a man, that he can be clean? Or he that is born of a woman, that he can be righteous?" Job 25:4 seems to repeat: "How then can man be righteous before God? How can he who is born of woman be clean?" Sin is more than just a matter of what we do. It's how we are!

David and his son Solomon attest to this truth. In Psalm 25:7 David talks about sins from youth, from childhood. David confesses in Psalm 51:5: "Behold, *I was brought forth in iniquity*, and in sin did my mother conceive me." David says that he was sinful as an infant even in the womb. In Psalm 58:3 he laments: "The wicked go astray *from the womb, they err from their birth*, speaking lies." In Ecclesiastes 7:20 Solomon says: "Surely there is not a righteous man on earth who does good and never sins."

If infants were really innocent of sin, why doesn't Scripture say this? Rather, the exact reverse is stated. There is "*nobody* so righteous on the earth", not even the newborn.

In his New Testament letters, the Apostle Paul frequently echoes the Psalms and Ecclesiastes. For example, he asserts in Romans 3:10-12 that "none is righteous, no, not one." Then in Romans 3:23 he states that "all have sinned and fall short of the glory of God." Again, the language of Scripture is ALL, with no exceptions. Romans 7:14-25 describes the Apostle's struggle with his sinful nature, his very own flesh. Ephesians

2:1-3 also speaks of man's sinful flesh and its desires. 1 Corinthians 15:50 is explicit: "I tell you this, brethren: flesh and blood cannot inherit the kingdom of God, nor does the perishable inherit the imperishable." So Paul can say: "The unspiritual man does not receive the gifts of the Spirit of God, for they are folly to him, and he is not able to understand them because they are spiritually discerned" (1 Corinthians 2:14). This is because man's very *will*, by nature, is corrupt and bound to sin according to Romans 8:7,8: "For the mind that is set on the flesh is hostile to God; it does not submit to God's law, *indeed it cannot; and those who are in the flesh cannot please God.*" Everyone is under the curse of sin and in need of God's saving work in their lives. "Everyone" means even the littlest.

Janet had remarked how peaceful, how innocent little Michael looked. This is not an easy matter for us in our day. Our society teaches us that people are by nature good. It's hard enough to believe that an *adult* is by nature sinful. Then to say that even small babies are sinful seems too much to bear. Yet that is exactly what the Bible teaches. Man's flesh, his nature, is sinful. The sinful flesh then expresses itself in sinful actions.

A person can't seem to beat an habitual sin. Two people are talking and one flies into a violent rage. A young person finds his or her thoughts quite often turning to lust. A brooding, self-centered depression settles over a life. Sometimes we manipulate other people—even unconsciously. As great as the urge to murder, as simple as a desire to lie, so sinful actions flow from a sinful flesh.

Man inherits this sinful flesh, ultimately, from Adam. As Romans 5:12 says: "Therefore as sin came into the world through one man and death through sin, and so death spread to all men because all men sinned." If babies were really sinless, this passage tracing our sin directly to Adam would simply have to be wrong. Sin would have nothing to do with Adam. Sin would only have to do with each man in and of himself.

In Romans 5, St. Paul traces our sin back to Adam. It seems unfair, doesn't it? Why should *all* people have to suffer for the one man's sin? God's system of justice is not always quite the same as ours. Is this a matter for us to complain to God about? Before we pass a too hasty judgment on God's system, perhaps we should see the full picture. On the same basis that sin was passed to all, so God grants his salvation from sin!

Romans 5 goes on to say that if by *one man* all were made sinners, so by Jesus Christ, *one man*, salvation was obtained for all. Even as Adam's one sin affected all of us, so the saving work of the one man, Jesus Christ, affects all of us. To deny the first denies the second.

> Those who reject the imputation of Adam's sin as an injustice are compelled, if they would be consistent, to declare the imputation of Christ's righteousness to be an injustice and to reject it; thus they take their stand outside the pale of Christianity.[1]

Romans 5:18-19 summarizes it all: "Then as *one* man's trespass led to condemnation for *all* men, so one man's act of righteousness leads to acquittal and life for *all* men. For as by one man's disobedience many were made sinners, so by one man's obedience many will be made righteous." Romans 5:15 says: "But the free gift is not like the trespass. For if many died through one man's trespass, how much more have the grace of God and the free gift in the grace of that one man Jesus Christ abounded for many." 1 Corinthians 15:22 also expresses this thought: "For as in Adam all die, so also in Christ shall all be made alive."

Although God's judgment on "original sin" may be a tough concept that doesn't quite seem fair, we can still praise the Lord. Even as Adam's sin brought us all death and a sinful nature, so Jesus brings us life. Why should one man's sin bring us all death? But then again, why should one righteous man's work bring us all life? That doesn't make sense on our scales either. But we can praise the Lord for it! One man's righteous act brought *me* life!

Original sin and baptism: John 3

But what connects original sin to infant baptism? First, because of original sin, babies too need to be saved. The Scriptures are very vocal about infant sin. Nor has God been silent about his saving plan for infants! John 3:5-8 can help us there. Verse 6 says: "That which is born of flesh is flesh, and that which is born of the Spirit is spirit." But wait a minute! What does "flesh" mean for John? Is it sinful? And what does "born" mean? In other words, how does this passage connect original sin to a need for water baptism?

John speaks of "flesh" in John 3:6. But for John, the Word, Jesus Christ, "became flesh" (John 1:14). Certainly the Word did not become sinful! Many writers have thus thought that John's "flesh" refers just to the realm of the earthly and the natural as opposed to the heavenly or the spiritual. In and of itself, "flesh" would not be sinful, that is, have original sin. But on the contrary, John *does* have a concept of original sin.

Each of the Gospels is concerned with the issue of Jesus as the Savior from sin. Each Gospel, however, tackles this theme from a different angle. John speaks of Jesus as the one who reveals the Father, who is the incarnate only-begotten Son (John 1:18). But as the people in John's Gospel meet Jesus, they come to a turning point in their lives. In the Gospel of John, sin reveals itself always in one's relation to Christ. Man either receives Jesus as the Son of God in the flesh, the Savior from sin, or rejects him (John 1:10-12).

Thus the Evangelist John deals in opposites: belief/ unbelief, light/darkness, flesh/spirit, from below/from above. All of these pairs contrast the earthly and natural with the divine and heavenly. John places "flesh" and "spirit" opposite each other in John 3. It's not enough to be born of flesh. A man must *also* be born of the Spirit. While *Christ's* flesh was not sinful, one need only see what happens to *man's* flesh. *Flesh without the Spirit is sinful flesh!* As the Pharisees judge "according to the flesh" they miss out on who Jesus is as the Savior (John 8:15). Throughout John's Gospel, when Christ is seen just according to the flesh, the person misses out on Christ as the Savior (for example, Nicodemus in John 3:3-8). Flesh when left to itself is lost .

When John places flesh in opposition to Spirit he is showing that flesh is not enough. The birth in flesh, without the birth in Spirit, leaves us in sin. And for John, there is no middle ground. The person in sin is a person opposed to the things of Christ. A man *must* be born from above. It is *necessary!* For until one is born from above, that person is left with sin clinging to his flesh. Such flesh can only lead *away* from the truth! So John emphasizes why we must be born *not* just of the flesh but from above (John 1:13)!

John is always trying to show that it's the spiritual level of things *in Christ* that counts. Why? Because apart from Christ the flesh is lost. What is this but original sin? The doctrine of original sin does not say that man's flesh *in itself* is evil (John 1:18). But it does say that sin cleaves to man's flesh, requiring the spiritual birth (John 3:3-8). It is sinful flesh that needed to be saved. So the Word became flesh.

Because of their sinful flesh, then, babies are in need

of spiritual birth, just as adults are. John 3:6 uses original sin as the explanation for the prior verse: ". . . unless one is born of water and the Spirit, he cannot enter the kingdom of God." But what does that phrase "of water and the Spirit" mean?

Some have said that the "water" here is figurative and not the water of baptism. But baptism is often referred to by such language. Nicodemus, to whom Jesus was speaking here, was a member of the Pharisees. The Gospel according to Luke says that the Pharisees did not receive baptism for the forgiveness of their sins (Luke 7:30). Nicodemus would have understood Christ's "new birth" in the sense of baptism. The Jews used such terms with their own convert baptism.[2] Not all the Jews, though, were sold on convert baptism. Perhaps Nicodemus's objection in John 3:4 was what he said to the Jews who baptized. But John was also writing his Gospel for an early Christian community that would have associated water with the regular baptism of new converts. Thus baptism would have been the obvious meaning of the term "water."

The context also indicates water baptism. After this discussion with Nicodemus, Jesus and his disciples went into Judea and baptized people (John 3:22). Verse 23 even speaks of John the Baptist baptizing. Water baptism thus forms the context of Jesus' talk with Nicodemus. This shows that the "water" with Nicodemus is baptism. Indeed, there is more to these verses than meets the eye.

Verses 22-30 of John 3 are mysteriously placed in the Gospel of John. The passage would really fit in better, thematically, right after the material on John the Baptist in John 1. The parallels are striking. The obvious common elements are John the Baptist and water baptism. Also, in John 1:19-21 the Baptist denies that he is the Christ. He denies that he is the Christ in 3:28. In

1:30, the Baptist says that Christ was before him (see also 3:28). In 1:30, John the Baptist says the Christ ranks before him, while in 3:30, the Baptist says that he himself must decrease.

But note also the parallels to the wedding at Cana. In 3:25, the dispute is over purification. In 2:6, Jesus uses purification jugs for his miracle. John 2 describes the wedding at Cana, and in John 3:29 we find more wedding imagery. Similar words are shared in the accounts. For example, "bridegroom" is common to both. The word "lesser" (wine) and (I must) "decrease" are related Greek words.

John 3:22-30 would seem to fit in better between 1:19-34 and 2:1-11, thematically. Why, then, is it here in chapter 3? The answer is that 3:22-30 along with 4:1,2 are strongly baptismal. After the talk with Nicodemus on "water and Spirit," this section serves to further and strengthen the *baptismal* theme in John 3:1-8. The inspired writer thus places the material here in order to teach the reader how to understand the talk with Nicodemus.

So, ". . . unless one is born of water and the Spirit, he cannot enter the kingdom of God." In other words, baptism is the means by which the Spirit works in man the spiritual birth that frees from the curse of his sinful flesh. The Greek word "*tis*" used here means "anyone" with no respect for age or status. That would include infants.

Some have thought that the passage speaks of *two* births, either one natural and one spiritual, or one by water baptism and one of the Spirit. But the phrase does not read "born *of* water *and* born *of* the Spirit" but rather reads "born *of* water *and* Spirit"—one act and event, not two.[3] So baptism is the means by which the effects of original sin in being "born of the flesh" are countered by being "born of the Spirit." F.D. Bruner develops this thought further:

Spiritually a man is born only once and that "of water and the Spirit." That is why baptism is the baptism of the Holy Spirit. Christian baptism is *one* (the single "of"), really a baptism ("of water"), and at the same time really spiritual ("and the Spirit").[4]

Finally, verse 8 in the context of John 3:5-7 shows why *infants* must be baptized and born of the Spirit. The Spirit "blows" wherever he wills whether we understand him or not. So it is with everyone born of the Spirit. Bruner writes of verse 8:

The descent of the Spirit in baptism remains a sovereign mystery and a wonder of grace. The only connection made for the Holy Spirit in this passage is with water. But *how* he relates himself to this water (coming immediately before, during, after?), or how and why he comes at all, is forbidden a too curious inquiry. Just as "the wind blows where it wills." . . . This is a clear warning against prescribing conditions (pattern) or evidences (pou) for the Spirit apart from his sovereign coming in Christ Jesus in baptism.[5]

The Spirit therefore can create faith in anyone as he pleases, adult or infant. He has promised, however, to work in the water of baptism. So when we baptize infants in view of their sinful flesh, we stand firmly on God's word in John 3:5 that one must be born of water and the Spirit to enter into God's kingdom. For the water and the Spirit work together *to reverse* the effects of man's sinful flesh (verse 6).

While the story of baptism began with the Fall and sin, it reaches its climax in Jesus and his saving work. Sin corrupts us all, by nature. But even as sin corrupts us all, so Jesus' saving work is for us all. Baptism takes all of Christ's saving work from centuries ago and makes it a reality for our lives today. In baptism, the effects of Adam's sin on the baby, indeed, on each of us, are countered.

But it's not just John 3:5-8 that tells us of the wonderful blessings that come with baptism. As we shall see, the Scriptures describe these blessings in *several* places.

2.

BAPTISM FOR SALVATION AND FORGIVENESS OF SINS

A pastor was teaching a class on baptism. He had just finished talking about how John 3:5-8 shows how baptism saves us from the sins of our flesh.[1]

Suddenly a woman raised her hand and asked, "Pastor, it seems hard to believe that applying water to someone is going to help them with eternity. How can *water* save?"

The emphasis on "water" almost stung.

"Sue, when we talk about being saved, we can only say what Scripture says. The Bible tells us that God works in his Word, his Holy Scriptures, to create faith, whenever the Bible is heard or read. But the Bible *also* says that baptism saves. God works in each of these 'means' to create faith."

"Well, I don't see why God couldn't just work faith directly. Why does he have to be tied down to water?"

"What God *could* have done is not for us to worry about. We can only go with how God *says* he is working."

"I just still have a hard time believing that water can save."

Symbol or reality?

How can water do such great things? That was exactly the question that many were asking at the time of the Reformation. In response, Luther once said about baptism:

> If God bade you pick up a stalk of grain or a strip of feather and, with his command, promised that through this act you should have forgiveness of all your sins, grace, and everlasting life, should you not accept that proposal with great pleasure and gratitude, love it, praise it, and esteem that stalk or feather a higher and holier possession than heaven and earth?[2]

Luther had a way of cutting to the heart of issues. God has simply associated his grace with baptism. Because of God's promises, and for that reason alone, baptism has become a rich treasure for the Christian! Whether for infants or adults, the Scriptures over and over again tell of the blessings of baptism. Baptism is God's gift to each of us!

Come with me on a journey through these Bible passages which speak of the blessings of baptism. And may his Spirit fill you with the wonderful assurances of His grace that came, or will come, to you in your baptism!

From the very earliest, the apostles stressed water baptism. Already at Pentecost, Peter says in Acts 2:38: "Repent, and be baptized every one of you in the name of Jesus Christ *for* (Greek: "*eis*") the forgiveness of your sins; and you shall receive the gift of the Holy Spirit." "So that," "into," or "for" are correct translations of the Greek preposition "*eis.*"[3] "*Eis*" means literally "into" here. In other words, baptism actually takes us "into" the forgiveness of our sins. That's the wonderful promise God has given us all in baptism!

Sadly, many Christians today believe that baptism is only a *symbol* of God's grace. But that word *"eis"* means much more than a mere symbol:

> If you say that you dip your hand into water, do you mean that it is a symbolical act whereby you confess that you have previously immersed your hand in water? Don't you mean that the act of dipping takes your hand into water?[4]

The context of verse 38 is also helpful. In verse 37 the people respond to Peter's words by asking him, "What shall we do?" The people were alarmed and crushed by their sin. They were responsible for the crucifixion of the Messiah (verse 36). "What shall we do?" To this Peter answered, "Repent and be baptized." It was *baptism* that took them into the forgiveness that they sought. Do you want to be certain of God's forgiveness? Then you too can hold firm to your water baptism as the proof that God has granted you his richest blessings and grace!

In Acts 22:16, Ananias came to Saul who was praying and said to him, "Rise and be baptized, and wash away your sins, calling on his name." The cleansing from sin takes place through the outward baptismal washing and with faith in the promises that come with water baptism. The passage does not say, "Since you have already received the forgiveness of your sins in the blood of Christ, arise and be baptized as a symbol of your faith before men." Rather, Saul was a penitent sinner in need of forgiveness. He was to receive the desired forgiveness *through baptism*.

But is the forgiveness offered in baptism a grace apart from the gospel of Jesus Christ? Isn't it the gospel alone that saves? How does water baptism fit in? Luther's *Small Catechism* says:

"It is certainly not the water that does such things,

but God's Word which is in and with the water and
faith which trusts this Word used with the water. For
without God's Word the water is just plain water and
not Baptism. But with this Word it is Baptism, that is,
a gracious water of life and a washing of rebirth by the
Holy Spirit."[5]

The power of baptism is in the gospel of Christ as
declared and decreed in his Word. Infant baptism rests
on nothing more than God's decree. He has simply
promised to work in the waters of baptism. Thus, it is
very evangelical. *Christ's* action alone is the power of
baptism.[6] The church baptizes in "the name of the
Father and of the Son and of the Holy Spirit" (Matthew
28:19). The power in baptism is not in mere water, but
water in connection with the Word of God, the gospel.

St. Paul also stresses over and over again God's saving
work in baptism. Paul speaks of baptism in Romans 6:3-
14. Note especially verses 3 and 4. There Paul writes:
"Do you not know that all of us who have been baptized
into Christ Jesus were baptized into his death? We were
buried therefore with him *by* baptism into death, so that
as Christ was raised from the dead by the glory of the
Father, we too might walk in the newness of life." In baptism our old sinful nature is nailed with Christ to the
cross (verse 6). In baptism we die with Christ and are
raised with him. Baptism takes us into an intimate and
special union with our Lord (*eis Christon Iesoun*). There
his saving work on the cross becomes a work for each of
us personally. For this reason, infants need baptism to
free them from the curse of their sinful flesh. Baptism is
not a mere symbol of God's forgiveness. Romans 6
emphasizes that *by means of baptism*, we share in
Christ's death and so live a new life.[7]

Colossians 2:12 speaks of the same truth: "and you
were buried with him *in baptism*, in which you were also
raised with him through faith in the working of God,

who raised him from the dead." Biblical scholar Oscar Cullman notes the parallel between baptism and our "dying with Christ":

> The parallelism between 'being baptized' and 'dying with Christ,' whose origin goes back to the life of Jesus at his own Baptism by John in Jordan, is traceable through the whole of the New Testament and is not limited to Romans 6:1ff. We find it first in Paul himself in 1 Corinthians 1:13, where baptism is clearly conceived as participation in the Cross of Christ. 'Was Paul crucified for you, or were ye baptized in the name of Paul?' Here the two expressions 'you were baptized' and 'another was crucified for you' are treated as synonymous. This uniformity of expression shows us also that it belongs to the essence of Christian Baptism in the New Testament, that it is Christ that operates, while the person baptized is the passive object of his deed.[8]

1 Corinthians 6:11 reminds us that it is by Jesus and *his* power that baptism works salvation. Baptism is not the work of men, but of God: "But you were washed, you were sanctified, you were justified in the name of the Lord Jesus Christ and in the Spirit of our God."[9] In 1 Corinthians 12:13 Paul says that people become members of the body of Christ, or the church, through baptism: "For we were all baptized into one body — Jews or Greeks, slaves or free, and all were made to drink of one Spirit."[10] Baptism brings us all together into Christ's body, his church!

Baptism is not the work of men, but of Christ. Paul *always* uses the passive voice in the verbs that denote baptism. The fact that humans administer baptism is not important (1 Corinthians 1:14-17). It is *God* who works in baptism (Ephesians 5:25-27; Colossians 2:13; Titus 3:5-7). And the power of baptism, as Paul shows, is in the finished work of the risen Christ.

But Paul speaks of the blessings of baptism also in Galatians 3:26-27: ". . . for in Christ Jesus you are all sons of God, through faith. For as many of you as were baptized into Christ have put on Christ." "To put on Christ" is to be covered as clothing covers our bodies. In baptism our sinful flesh is covered.

Some think that Paul's words "do you not know" shows that he was writing only to adults. So is baptism only for them? Rather, Paul was writing to those who could read and hear to remind them of what had happened in their baptism. So also children, when older, need to be reminded of *their* baptisms and of its meaning for their lives. We *all* need to be constantly reminded of the blessings God gave each of us in our baptism!

Have you ever wondered why there are sponsors at baptisms? This is the reason! Infants need to be reminded of their baptism when they are older. If you are a sponsor, that is your job, along with the parents. You can testify that the child was properly baptized and you can help that little one come to terms with the meaning of that baptism for his or her spiritual life.

In Ephesians 5:25-27 are the well-known words often heard at marriages: "Husbands, love your wives, as Christ loved the church and gave himself up for her that he might sanctify her, having cleansed her by the washing of water with the word. . . ." Husbands are to love their wives as the Lord loved the church. Our Lord gave his life for the church and now conveys his love and forgiveness in baptism. Literally, the text reads "by means of the washing of water, in the word."[11] "Washing with water" is a metaphor for the cleansing from sin in baptism. Paul did not write that Christ first cleansed the church by his Word and then symbolized it all by the washing of baptism. Rather, it is by baptism, the washing of water, his church is cleansed.

In Titus 3:5-7 it is written: ". . . and he saved us, not because of deeds done by us in righteousness, but in virtue of his own mercy, by *the washing* of regeneration and the renewal in the Holy Spirit." The definite article shows that the washing referred to is baptism. Further, the terms used here are similar to those used in Acts 22:16 and John 3:5. Those passages are treating water baptism. People are saved from their sins by the washing given in baptism by the Holy Spirit.

A means of grace

But wait a minute! So God promises his grace with water baptism. But why? Why water baptism *in addition to* God's forgiveness given through the hearing of the word about Christ? It's as simple as sin. A person convicted by sin needs that extra testimony to God's forgiveness. In the tangibles of water or of bread and wine, the person crushed by his or her sins and weak in faith encounters the truly superabundant riches of God's grace in Christ. God wanted men to be absolutely sure of his forgiveness. So he promises his grace also with tangible elements like the water .

Indeed, it is quite in keeping with God's dealings with mankind that water should be used as a vehicle of God's grace. God offered his blessings and grace in the Old Testament often with material components. An excellent example is the case of Naaman. In 2 Kings 5, Elisha instructed Naaman who was suffering from leprosy (verse 10): "Go and wash in the Jordan seven times, and your flesh shall be restored, and you shall be clean." Naaman became angry with God's instructions through the prophet (verse 11): "Behold, I thought that he would surely come out to me, and stand, and call on the name of the Lord his God, and wave his hand over the place, and cure the leper." And so Naaman left Elisha. Later (verse 13), Naaman's servants spoke with him: "My father, if the prophet had commanded you to do some great thing, would you not have done it ? How much rather, then, when he says to you, 'Wash and be clean'?" And so Naaman washed and was miraculously cleansed of his leprosy.

By nature, man resists the gospel of grace when it is offered. Naaman resisted this prophetic "form" of the water baptism yet to come. Naaman resisted physical healing even as many resist and reject the grace of God, the spiritual cleansing from sin, offered in the water of baptism. God has simply told us in his Word that he works the forgiveness of sins in baptism. We must not argue with God but simply trust the Word of God in baptism.

The prototypes of baptism were for the forgiveness of sins. Old Testament washings were for cleansing before God. The Jews' convert baptism was to purify the Gentiles from the uncleanness of paganism. Finally, even John's baptism was for the forgiveness of sins. As Mark 1:4 says: "John the baptizer appeared in the wilderness, preaching a baptism of repentance *for* (*eis*) the forgiveness of sins." Luke 3:3 concurs: "[John the Baptist] went into all the region about the Jordan, preaching a baptism of repentance *for* (*eis*) the forgiveness of sins."

What, then, was the difference between Christ's baptism and John the Baptist's? Matthew 3:11, Luke 3:16, and John 1:33 show that Christ's baptism would be a baptism by the Holy Spirit. So in Acts when the Spirit falls on people, water baptism is usually found in the context of the events.[12] The Spirit comes either right before, during, or after the water baptism, but both are always found together. This would be expected given the words of John 3:8.[13] The post-Pentecostal nature of the Spirit's operation is the key difference between Christ's and John's baptisms. That even John's baptism, however, was for the forgiveness of sins shows that Christian baptism has saving power.

The Bible's teaching on baptism is not limited to Paul. St. Peter writes in respect to Noah: "Baptism, which corresponds to this, now saves you" (1 Peter 3:20,21). Noah's salvation through the flood of wrath in the ark by *water* foreshadowed water baptism. Water drew the line of separation between the old world and the new world after the Flood. Water delivered Noah from the old world into the new one. So water baptism also delivers us from the world of sin into the new world in Christ. In water baptism, we are spared from the judgment that the Flood prefigures.

According to Peter, baptism does not save us by washing dirt from our bodies. Rather, baptism provides us, through Christ's rising from the dead, a "good conscience" before God. Peter clearly says "baptism saves you." So are we now to say that the water of baptism does not save?

Mark 16:16 states: "He who believes and is baptized will be saved." The passage says that one is saved if he believes and is baptized. The passage does *not* say that one must first believe and be saved, and then be baptized. No, it is by belief *and* baptism that one is saved. In Acts 8:36-38, the eunuch had a repentant faith that desired baptism. So we see that repentant faith leads to baptism.

In Acts 2, Peter calls the people to respond and be baptized to be saved. Baptism without belief does not save. That was made clear in the case of Simon Magus in Acts 8:9-25. Therefore baptism, as a means of grace, imparts salvation and must be received by faith. But it is still by belief *and* baptism that one is saved.

The Bible says that it is through baptism that our sins are covered and washed away. God has entrusted baptism to his church as a "means of grace." We must not deny infants and children God's saving means. God has said in the Scriptures that he will save through baptism. Infants need to be saved too. Thus the infant needs baptism! Given the wonderful promises connected with baptism, why would parents want to keep children from the waters that save?

The necessity of baptism

Is baptism necessary? The Scriptures say *yes*! (See John 3:6 and elsewhere.) While in Mark 16:16, it is *unbelief* that damns, true belief would lead one to be baptized. Simply because of the promise of cleansing from sin, true belief would lead to baptism. It is the repentant sinner who does not plan to be baptized who is to be questioned. As Martin Luther has written: "The unbaptized believer is not damned. He stands condemned who does not believe." He who does not believe the Scriptures on the need or command to be baptized stands condemned. Baptism is necessary only because God grants his grace through it. Why would anyone want to pass up the free gift of God's grace? Why would anyone keep another from the love of God given each of us in baptism?

But if baptism is necessary, what about the individual in Luke 23:43, the thief on the cross? Wasn't he saved without baptism? Romans 10:17 says that faith comes from hearing the Word. Perhaps the thief on the cross did not have the chance to be baptized as the Scriptures require. In Mark 16:16, while baptism is necessary, it's *unbelief* that damns. But how can anyone say for sure that this person was *not* baptized? That would be mere assumption as well. Perhaps the thief on the cross had taken part in John the Baptist's baptism. John 3:22 and 4:12 show that many people were already baptized in the course of Jesus' ministry. Finally, baptism was for-

mally instituted for the church only *after* Christ's resurrection (Matthew 28:18-20). Thus, the church and any
who seek to enter it need to be faithful to Christ's baptism. Passages such as Luke 23:43 are simply *silent* on
the matter of baptism.

Some say that infant baptism is not needed in Christian homes because of 1 Corinthians 7:14: "For the unbelieving husband is consecrated through his wife [a
Christian], and the unbelieving wife is consecrated
through her husband. Otherwise, your children would be
unclean, but as it is they are holy."

Because of the common misconception that Christians
need not baptize their infants, parents often delay their
children's baptisms. They believe that their children are
saved since they as parents are Christian. Is this Bibli-
cally sound?

Some scholars feel that it is. Paul says the believing
spouse sanctifies the unbelieving one through the marriage relationship. Paul presents, as proof of this, the
holiness of the children. A connection is drawn between
the children and the unbelieving spouse. If the unbaptized unbelieving spouse is sanctified by the believing
spouse, wouldn't the same apply also to the children?
The relationship to the believing spouse, some contend,
would be enough. This would easily apply also to the
children of Christian homes where both spouses believe.
If the children are sanctified by the belief of the parents,
baptism would be unnecessary. That would seem to
mean that the children of converts should be baptized,
but not children born into Christian homes.

Is such reasoning valid? First of all, how this passage
applies to baptism is by no means clear. The passage
doesn't really say anything about baptism. Further, is
this an argument to be wielded against infant baptism
per se? The interpretation of 1 Corinthians 7:14 would
only apply to the children of Christian homes. It would

not argue against infant baptism in general, especially in the case of the children of converts.

Joachim Jeremias once thought that this passage showed that only the children of converts should be baptized. The children of Christian homes would not need baptism, being "in holiness." But he was later forced to change his mind. While Jewish boys were born "in holiness," they were still circumcised. If baptism is the circumcision of Christ (Colossians 2:11f), then this passage (1 Corinthians 7:14) cannot rule out the baptism of believers' children.[14] But further:

> Even in the case of an unbelieving husband in a mixed marriage, the fact that he was made holy by his marriage to a Christian partner did not make it unnecessary for him to be converted and baptized! *We must accordingly be silent with the conclusion that 1 Corinthians 7:14c bears no reference to baptism.*[15]

To say that the children are made holy and so do not need baptism implies that the believing spouse does not need baptism either. Would not the spouse also be included in the sanctification of the home? Being consistent, then, to not baptize the infants of a Christian home renders the baptism of certain adults unnecessary. This flagrantly contradicts the Scriptures which say that one must *believe* and *be baptized* to be saved.

An unbeliever is not automatically saved simply because he or she has a believing spouse. Rather, being "holy" or "consecrated" points to the blessings of such a union. The unbeliever is exposed to the believing spouse's faith and life. Such godly witness may eventually lead the unbeliever to faith. But, once again, it will be the Holy Spirit working through the Word and baptism who actually creates the faith.

On the other hand, the passage can also be viewed as evidence *for* infant baptism in Christian homes. Only the children of Christian parents were baptized in the Apostolic church since only these children would be given a Christian upbringing "in the nurture and admonition of the Lord" in the sanctified holiness of a Christian home.

If only one of the parents was a Christian, the home was sanctified. Thus the children should have been baptized. For example, in the household baptisms in Acts, we shall see that it was the faith of the head of the household that was the basis for the entire family's baptism. It was not enough that only one member of the household believed and was baptized. The sanctification of the household was not enough in these cases. It must lead to the *whole* family's baptism! The concern is for the salvation of the *entire* household. So also then in 1 Corinthians 7:14, the sanctity of the home by the believing spouse *intensifies* the need for the children to be baptized. All the household is to be saved. God's blessings in baptism are for *each and every one of us*!

Baptism "for the dead"

Another passage that has been much discussed is 1 Corinthians 15:29: "Otherwise, what do people mean by being baptized *on behalf of* (*huper*) the dead? If the dead are not raised at all, why are people baptized on their behalf (huper)?" Some have sought to argue from 1 Corinthians 15:29 that there is a baptism for the benefit of those who have died. If so, may the church baptize for those infants and others who died without baptism?

The phrase "for the dead" (*huper ton nekron*) is better translated "with a view to the dead," according to R.C.H. Lenski. If Paul meant that baptizing the living helped the dead, he would have used different wording (*huper nekron*). Rather, believers receive baptism to prepare for "*the* dead." Baptism provides us hope for *after* death. For the sake of when we die, we receive baptism. If baptism doesn't save, "Else what shall we do?"[16] Further, the concept of being baptized for those who have died is a concept alien to the rest of the Scriptures. Obscure passages in Scripture must be explained by those that are clear. A doctrine of baptism for the dead cannot be drawn from this passage alone. The context of the passage, instead, points to the coming resurrection of the dead. Baptism is thus "with a view to" the dead, that is, *the* dead who are Christian. For there is no hope in baptism if the dead do not rise.

Thus we see even in 1 Corinthians 15:29 how Paul is showing the wonderful benefits of water baptism as a preparation for life after death! I think you can now see that the Scriptures have a great deal to say about the blessings of water baptism. Baptism is no mere symbol of God's forgiveness. It is an *instrument* of God's forgiveness. It is a precious gift that we can all cling to when burdened by our sinfulness. It is God's free gift for all, even as salvation itself!

The next time you find yourself crushed by a sin or your own shortcomings as a sinful human being, don't just despair over the sickness of sin. Take a few moments right away to praise God for your baptism. Your baptism took you "into Christ." Being "in Christ" we are God's children and have received his forgiveness. So we have special rights as his heirs. We can pray in faith trusting God simply because of what his Word promises to us in baptism. If you have a baptized child, take a moment to also thank God that the same gift washes your child of his or her sins as well. And then go back to overcome that troubling sin. You can work on it in the victory that God gives each of us in baptism. In baptism we too share in the victory of Christ's cross over sin and death. We are forgiven of all our sins and granted the power of the Holy Spirit. And you can be confident that even your littlest ones share in that same victory!

3.

INFANT FAITH AND BAPTISM (PART I)

"Your church baptizes babies? But why?"

"We believe that God saves them through baptism," replied Theresa.

"But doesn't the Bible say he that *believes* and is baptized shall be saved?"

"Well, sure, but . . . ." Theresa wasn't really sure what to say as Mike went on.

"How can a baby believe? A baby can't accept Jesus as its Savior. A baby doesn't even know what baptism means!"

"But how else are they going to be saved?" asked Theresa.

"Maybe God's got a special plan for babies. But it can't be baptism. Baptism's not any good unless you believe. And a baby's not old enough to know anything about the Lord." . . .

Can babies believe?

How can a little baby believe in the Lord? And yet

Scripture says: "Whoever *believes* in him shall not perish but have eternal life" (John 3:16). Mark 16:16 says one must *believe* and be baptized. Acts 2:38 says: "*Repent* and be baptized." How do infants "repent" or "believe"? Aren't they unconscious of such things?

More often than not, this is the toughest stumbling block that many Christians have to infant baptism. Even those who believe in the doctrine may find themselves scratching their heads on this one. Yet the question is inevitable. Everyone seems to be asking it.

The situation wasn't helped much by Swiss theologian Karl Barth. Considered by some the premier theologian of the century, Barth wrote against infant baptism:

> We have not left it [infant baptism] out artificially. There has been no place at which there could even be any question of thinking that the candidate to whom we have constantly referred as a partner of the community in baptism might be an infant, an *unconscious* child. . . . Indeed, we have thought it could be regarded as self-evident that in the work of baptism one has to presuppose . . . human beings who are *capable of thought* and action and who may be summoned as such to conversion, obedience, hope, and the *decision* of faith.[1]

How can an unconscious infant accept the benefits of baptism?

Thus, for Barth, infant baptism is an "astonishing possibility." Baptism is only valid when accompanied by faith or belief (Mark 16:16). The Scriptures are clear that faith must go along with the baptism. So why baptize one who is incapable of such faith, according to Barth?

Let us assume for a moment that infants are unable to believe in the Lord. Then that means that *infants cannot disbelieve*! They cannot consciously reject the gospel! Now consider how predominantly infants figure all through Scripture. They are among the "all nations" of the world, spoken of in Matthew 28:19. They are part of God's covenant with Abraham (Genesis 17:10-12). They figure heavily in Jesus' teaching in the Gospels. And if infants can't reject the gospel, surely that casts the matter in a different light. Luther writes in his *Large Catechism*:

> . . . we are not primarily concerned whether the baptized person believes or not, for in the latter case baptism does not become invalid. Everything depends upon the Word and commandment of God. This, perhaps, is a rather subtle point, but it is based upon what I have already said, that Baptism is simply water and God's Word in and with each other; that is, when the Word accompanies the water, Baptism is valid, even though faith be lacking. For my faith does not constitute Baptism but receives it. Baptism does not become invalid even if it is wrongly received or used, for it is bound not to our faith but to the Word.[2]

Baptism is simply water used according to and with the Word of God. Luther explains that baptism is a once-for-all objective event in one's life. Even if the infant did not believe, the baby would still be properly baptized. Infant baptism is, then, valid in and of itself.

But still, the benefits of baptism must be subjectively appropriated by faith. If the infant could not believe, the child would not benefit from the baptism right away. So Luther writes elsewhere: "If we cannot supply a better answer to this question and prove that little children themselves believe and have a faith of their own, then my honest advice and judgment are to abstain. . . ."[3]

So we come back to the basic question: "*Can* infants possess the faith their baptism requires?"

Yes, since faith is entirely the work of God

Many Christians speak of the day or hour when they "accepted" the Lord. Karl Barth spoke of the "decision" of faith. Billy Graham calls his evangelism magazine *Decision*. For all of them, faith is a conscious acceptance of Jesus Christ after being old enough to understand the gospel. Infants cannot have such a faith. They're too young to accept the gospel. How many parents have delayed their child's baptism because they wanted it to be the child's own decision?

But this way of thinking puts the burden of salvation on man and his own works. Salvation becomes man's decision to accept God and his love for us rather than God's acceptance of man. At heaven's gates a man could say, "God, you should let me into your heaven because I chose to accept your plan of salvation."

Scripture, however, teaches a different view of faith. Faith is given *by the grace of God* (Ephesians 2:8). Ephesians 2:9,10 explains: ". . . not because of works, lest any man should boast. *For we are his workmanship, created in Christ Jesus for good works, which God prepared beforehand, that we should walk in them.*" In other words, God "creates" the man in Christ Jesus. Faith is not "accepted" but received.

Over and over again, Scripture bears this out. Jesus told his disciples in John 15:16: "*You did not choose me, but I chose you and appointed you that you should go and bear fruit and that your fruit should abide*; so that whatever you ask the Father in my name, he may give it to you." The disciples didn't "accept" the Lord. Rather Christ came to them and chose them as his own. Ephesians 1:4,5 states: ". . .even as *he chose us* in him before the foundation of the world, that we should be holy and blameless before him. He *destined* us in love to be his sons through Jesus Christ, according to the purpose of his will." Romans 9:9-24 teaches that God makes the Christian righteous and not vice versa. As Romans 9:16 puts it, "So it depends not upon man's will or exertion, but upon God's mercy." Paul categorically denies that man could want Christ or accept him.

Sin is so great that it even enslaves man's very *will*: "For the mind that is set on the flesh is hostile to God; it does not submit to God's law, indeed it cannot" (Romans 8:7). In Romans 7:14-20, Paul talks about the struggle he has even *as a Christian* to live in the Lord. Sin totally rules the flesh and man's will until God brings one to faith and thus restores the Christian's will to live a godly life.

People like to speak of an "age of accountability" when the child is able to understand the things of the faith. Consider 1 Corinthians 2:14: "The unspiritual man does not receive the gifts of the Spirit of God, for they are folly to him, and he *is not able to understand* them because they are spiritually discerned." The Scripture says that mankind, by nature, whether infant or adult, is *unable* to "accept" or welcome the things of God. Man, of himself, is even unable to *understand* the things of God.

Consider also the following Bible passages:

Ezekiel 12:2: "Son of man, you dwell in the midst of a rebellious house, *who have eyes to see, but see not, who have ears to hear, but hear not.*"

Jeremiah 6:10: "To whom shall I speak and give warning, that they may hear? Behold, their ears are closed, *they cannot listen*; behold, the Word of the Lord is to them an object of scorn; they take no pleasure in it."

Zechariah 7:11: "But they refused to hearken, and turned a stubborn shoulder, and stopped their ears that they might not hear."

Matthew 13:15: "For this people's heart has grown dull, and their ears are heavy of hearing, and their eyes they have closed, lest they should perceive with their eyes, and hear with their ears, and understand with their heart, and turn for me to heal them." (See also Acts 28:26,27; Isaiah 6:10.)

2 Timothy 4:4: ". . . and will turn away from listening to the truth and wander into myths."

Man is oriented, because of his sinful flesh, *against* the gospel of Jesus Christ. So faith must be received. It is a gift given without anything done on the part of the person. Man is simply passive and God active in the creation of faith.

But wait a minute! Revelation 3:20 says: "Behold, I stand at the door and knock; if any one hears my voice and opens the door, I will come in to him and eat with him, and he with me." So doesn't the individual have to "open the door" to him? But every passage on choosing to do good or to "open the door" is *in the context of those already* Christian or numbered in *the house* of *Israel.* The words of Revelation 3:20 are to those *already* saved in the *church* of Laodicea. The works in the Christian life, the confession, the living, the changes *follow* the creation of faith by God's grace. The Christian life that flows out of God's saving work is *then* a continual opening of the doors of our lives to the Lord. We must let him work his will more fully in our daily life of faith.

It is difficult these days to see faith as that which is purely received. Too often, Christians speak of "accepting" the Lord. How we speak about things molds how we think. It's no wonder then that adults have a hard time with infant baptism. After all, an infant can't "accept" the Lord Jesus. But it is amazing how many who understand the Scriptures on this also use the language of "accept" and "open the door" to our salvation. This is tragic. As Christians we would do well to try to mold our language into accord with God's Word. While an infant cannot "accept" the Lord, an infant can *receive* him!

Since faith is entirely a result of a decision by God for the sake of man, it's easy to see that God can work faith even in infants. Faith is a miracle in any person and must be since the natural man *cannot* receive the things of God's Spirit (1 Corinthians 2:14). The disciples asked Jesus in Matthew 19:25: "Who then can be saved?" What was Jesus' answer in the following verse? "With men this is *impossible, but with God all things are possible.*" Jesus says that men cannot be saved by anything of themselves, but God can do anything. God can create faith in infants just as he can create faith in the rich man in Matthew 19 as he so chooses. So Colossians 2:12 says that the faith that is to go along with baptism is "produced by the power of God." God will simply create faith in the infant.

John 3:5 says that *all* must be born *of* water *and* Spirit. Is man to say that God's Spirit cannot create faith in infants? John 3:8 says: "The wind blows where it wills, and you hear the sound of it, but you do not know whence it comes or whither it goes; so it is with every one who is born of the Spirit." John 3:8 warns against trying to set limits or boundaries over the work of the Spirit that is promised in baptism.

The Spirit meets man where he is at through the Word. The Word opens man's ears so he can hear. The Word gives man sight to see God's truth. The power of the Word can meet the infant in the same supernatural way as it meets the adult. Infants and adults are all equally incapable of faith of themselves.

Baptism has been given that we may receive the kingdom of God. Infants should be baptized in *accordance with scriptural teaching that baptism is for salvation.* The infant *needs* baptism to enter into God's kingdom (John 3:6-8). Why deny baptism to the infant or little child who by the power of God can also believe? When one thinks of the wonderful blessings that come in baptism, who wouldn't baptize a small baby?

Yes, since infants are examples of receiving the faith

The evidence for infant faith reaches into the very heart of Matthew's Gospel. The Evangelist Matthew weaves the motif of the kingdom of God through his Gospel. To enter God's kingdom is to enter into the elect who will inherit *heaven and eternal life* (Matthew 24:34,35; John 3:3; 18:36; Acts 14:22; 1 Corinthians 15:50; James 2:5). In his talk with the disciples on "who is the greatest in the kingdom of heaven," Jesus called a little child (Matthew 18:1,2). The disciples' argument was over status and prestige in the kingdom. Jesus set the little child up as an object lesson for the disciples. He told them that they must become as the little child to make it into heaven.

Salvation is only by faith in Christ, according to the words of Jesus and his Scriptures (Mark 16:16; John 3:15; 10:9; 11:25; Acts 4:12; Romans 5:1; Galatians 3:24; Ephesians 2:8,9; Philippians 3:9). Yet this little child's faith was a model for the disciples. If one wishes to be great in the kingdom, then it can only be by the quality of one's faith. And the faith spoken of here is not the kind that is self-conscious, but rather is completely trusting and leaning on the grace of God. The disciples in Matthew 18 were self-conscious of their faith. "Look at my faith," they were really saying. "No," Jesus responded, "you must become as a little child to get into God's kingdom."

A look at the people with great faith in Jesus' journeys shows that they were anything but conscious of the greatness of their faiths. In Matthew 8:5-13, the Roman centurion confessed: "Lord, I am not worthy to have you come under my roof." The centurion didn't say: "Do this because of my faith." Rather, it was his humble awareness of sin for which Christ praised him.

In Matthew 9:19-22, the woman just touched his garment in the hope of healing. The woman had no concern with her own greatness. Her focus was entirely upon the Savior whom she knew could heal.

The Pharisees, on the other hand, were very conscious of their own faith and obedience to the Law. Jesus had much to say about *their* faiths: "They do all their deeds to be seen by men" (Matthew 23:5).

In Matthew 15:21-28, Jesus praised the faith of a woman whose daughter was possessed. The woman humbled herself before him, even counting herself among the dogs who eat the crumbs at their master's table. Jesus called this woman an example of faith.

Neither Jesus nor the Scriptures ever claim that true faith must be conscious of itself or rational. Faith is not the same as conscious reason. However, there is a connection. Faith will also express itself in a person's whole life. That means if a person is *capable* of conscious thought and reason, faith must express itself there. So true faith is never concerned with itself but is simply a soul resting in God's grace. For an infant or small child such faith would be easy. Adults tend to consciously rest on their own strength, rather than on God's grace.[4] It is the simple humility of the child that is great in the kingdom of heaven according to Matthew 18:4: "Whoever humbles himself like this child, he is the greatest in the kingdom of heaven."

Jesus does not just say, "You must become humble as this child." In Matthew 18:5-6, he continues: "Whoever receives one such child in my name receives me." Who can say that such a little child *does not* have faith? Christ lives in people by the faith that the Holy Spirit creates. The only way a person could receive Christ in receiving this child is if Christ is already living by faith in the child.

The child that Christ used for an example is a *"little child."* The Greek word is *"paidion."* This word refers to *infants*, babies and very, very small children. To welcome this small child that Jesus used as an example is to welcome him.

Jesus goes on: ". . . but whoever causes one of these little ones who believe in me to sin, it would be better for him to have a great millstone fastened round his neck and to be drowned in the depth of the sea." "Little ones" in the Greek is *"mikroon"* which "refers to the class of children under four years old and according to both Hebrew and New Testament usage has special reference to the 'littlest,' namely the infants."[5] If all this were not enough, Jesus further expounds in verse 10: "See that you do not despise one of these little ones; for I tell you that in heaven their angels always behold the face of my Father who is in heaven."

Note also that Jesus is admonishing . . . *his disciples*! And he warns of punishment for offending these "little ones who believe in me." In other words, not only is the little child an example of faith to the disciples who were so busy with their own faiths (verse 3), but they are even admonished not to offend any of these little ones who believe. Isn't this what adult disciples do when they look at their own faiths and then refuse to baptize the "little ones" since they don't see how infants can believe? These words of Jesus apply to his adult disciples, both then and *today*.

The word Christ used for "believe" in the phrase "these little ones who *believe* in me" is *"pisteuo"* which means: *"to have faith* (in, upon, or with respect to, a person or thing) . . . by implication to *entrust* (especially one's spiritual well-being to Christ): believe, commit (to trust), put in trust with."[6] Yes, the "believe" used here is the same one used in John 3:15-36. *"Pisteuo"* is the standard word for "believe" in the New Testament, the saving belief in Jesus Christ. In Matthew 18:6, Jesus quite openly and explicitly declares in the phrase "these little ones who believe in me" that children *under four years* of age *can believe* in him.

Who are *we* to question with our human understanding and reason the possibility of infant faith when Jesus so clearly accepts it? The Lord says they can believe. Dare the adult Christian disagree and fall under the curse of those who offend these "little ones who believe"? Dare the Church deny them the full rights of a believer given in baptism, namely the cleansing from sin? By these warnings, Jesus wants to impress on adults how important the little ones are to him.

Jesus did not conclude his teaching on the little children with Matthew 18:10. He reinforced his teaching on infant faith with the parable of the lost sheep. And Jesus applies it all to the little children. "So it is not the will of my Father who is in heaven that one of these little ones should perish" (verse 14). In the very next chapter, Matthew 19, Jesus warned the disciples sternly: "Let the children come to me, and do not hinder them; for to such as these belongs the kingdom of heaven."[7]

In the context of the prior chapter, the quality Jesus was praising children for is clear. Heaven and the kingdom of God belong to such as these because of the nature of their humble faith (Matthew 18:3,5,6). Jesus rebuked his disciples for keeping the children of faith away. In the same way, adults today often keep little children away from him. The danger of Matthew 18:6 also still applies. Self-conscious adults tend to rationalize faith. But faith in anyone is a miracle of God. For it is in the context of the little children who believe, which so permeates Matthew 18 and the early part of 19, that Jesus says in regard to saving faith in verse 26: *"With men this is impossible, but with God all things are possible."*

Some Christians think that infants are *already* in a state of grace. But none of the Gospel accounts of Christ and the little children support such an idea. These infants are examples of how to receive God's kingdom. But *not all infants have received the kingdom.* Hoffman writes:

> Jesus emphasizes such and thereby refers to those children who are brought to him. He does not express as a general rule that "the Kingdom of God belongs to children," but that it belongs to such children as are brought to Him.[8]

In other words, if infants are to receive the kingdom, adults must *bring them* to Jesus. This is done in baptism, where God works faith in the infant and saves the child. We can now see why Jesus warned the disciples so sternly with regard to the children. Jesus has entrusted the spiritual welfare of the little ones to adults.

Finally, Luke's version (18:15-17) of the same events has much to add to Matthew's account. In verse 15, the term *"brephae"* is used in the Greek. Matthew's *"paidion"* refers to all those under four years of age including the infants. But *"brephae"* refers *only* to infants. The people brought to Jesus *infants!* The disciples were rebuking the people when Jesus spoke the stern words: "Let the children come to me, and do not hinder them; for to such belongs the kingdom of God. Truly, I say to you, whoever does not receive the kingdom of God like a child shall not enter it." Again, the word for "receive" is not in the future tense, but the Greek aorist, denoting a completed action at a certain point in time. Christ said more than that *these* infants were able to receive the kingdom. They had received it! And thus they became examples to adults of how to receive God's gifts.[9]

Luke also records the words of Christ about the rich man of Matthew in the same context of infant faith (Luke 18:15-17,27). "What is impossible with men is possible with God" (verse 27). Faith which saves in adults must be of the quality of infant faith. By such words in Matthew and Luke (see also Mark 10:13-27), Christ went out of his way openly to show that infants can believe.

Yes, because the Bible openly says that infants can believe

The Gospels abound in proof that even babies can believe. In Luke 10:21, Christ says: "I thank thee, Father, Lord of heaven and earth, that thou hast hidden these things from the wise and understanding and revealed them to babes; yea, Father, for such was thy gracious will." The Greek word "*nepios*" here refers to babies and very, very small children, those "not speaking" yet. This passage surely strains the present day concept of an "age of accountability." *Nepios* can also be used figuratively in the sense of the "simple-minded." Such are those to whom the Father reveals his truth. Faith is not dependent on human wisdom or intelligence. Faith would then be a human action when the Word says that it is the work of God. Human understanding of the gospel is not enough. God reveals the truth of his gospel to whomever he will, including the little children, by his Spirit (1 Corinthians 2:14-16). God miraculously reveals his truth to even the little baby. Faith does not depend on an age when one can "understand" the words of the gospel. These are not the words of modern psychology and rationalism, but of Scripture. It is as in I Peter 2:2: "*Like newborn babes*, long for the pure spiritual milk, that by it you may grow up to salvation."

Such passages are not just in the Gospels. For instance, Psalm 22:9,10 says: "Yet thou art he who took me from the womb; thou didst keep me safe upon my mother's breasts. Upon thee was I cast from my birth, and since my mother bore me thou hast been my God." Psalm 71:5,6 states: "For thou, O Lord, art my hope, my trust, O Lord, from my youth. Upon thee have I leaned from my birth; thou art he who took me from my mother's womb. My praise is continually of thee." So the Old Testament declares that children *from birth* can trust and believe in the Lord.

People say infants cannot confess their sin or believe in Jesus Christ as Lord and Savior. Would they say on similar grounds that an infant cannot praise God? Matthew 21 follows on the heels of Jesus and the small children in Matthew 18 and 19. In Matthew 21:15,16 the Jewish Bible scholars disapproved of the children in the temple shouting, "Hosanna to the Son of David." What was Jesus' response? "Yes; have you never read, 'Out of the mouth of *babes and sucklings thou hast brought perfect praise*'?" *Infants* can *praise* God. So why couldn't infants also confess Christ as Lord? A man can praise God as Lord only if the Spirit has so moved him (1 Corinthians 12:3). Romans 8:1-17 says that "all who are led by the Spirit of God are sons of God" (verse 14). This passage teaches that it is the Spirit who brings man to Christ and to the point where he can say, "Abba Father." Hence, babies at the breast praising him is only possible by the Spirit who has created faith.

Luke 1:15 says that John the Baptist "will be filled with the Holy Spirit, even from his mother's womb."

Luke 1:41 and 44 speak of John the Baptist's belief while in his mother's womb: "And when Elizabeth heard the greeting of Mary, the babe leaped in her womb. . . . 'For behold, when the voice of your greeting came to my ears, the babe in my womb leaped for joy.'"[10] Joy is a fruit of the Spirit's work (Galatians 5:22). Adults can truly rejoice and praise God that he works belief even in small children and infants.

Yes, because faith is the only way to be saved

Finally, faith in Christ and baptism is the *only* way to be saved. If infants cannot believe and so have faith, how else can they be saved from the effects of sin? Are those who deny infant faith saying that no infant can be saved because the child is not old enough to have true faith? Is not this implied in the denial of infant faith? Scripture says that it is only by faith in Christ that one is saved (Acts 4:12; Ephesians 2:8,9). If the infant cannot believe, baptism would be of no value to the infant. But what then is of value to the infant? Fortunately, the Scriptures are quite clear: infants also believe and receive faith. The forgiveness of sins in baptism must be for them as well.

4.

INFANT FAITH AND BAPTISM
(PART II)

We have seen in the Scriptures that infants can possess the faith that baptism requires since:

1. Faith is entirely the work of God.
2. Infants are examples of how to receive faith.
3. The Scriptures are explicit on infant faith.
4. Faith is the only way to be saved.

While this takes us a long way, no doubt there still remain a number of unanswered questions. For example, it's wonderful to say that infants *can* believe, but which infants actually *do* believe? So then, how do we know which babies to baptize? After all, isn't faith supposed to go *before* baptism? And if infants are saved in baptism, why do so many end up such poor witnesses of their baptism? Finally, what about the option of blessing infants instead?

Which infant do we baptize?

Baptism *requires* faith to be of any value. Which

infant has such a faith? If infants cannot confess their beliefs in the same way as older people, how does one know if a certain infant believes? One caution, right away, is that no one can judge who has faith and who does not. Even with adults, there is no absolute way of knowing whether the person who says he believes truly believes or not. The church must accept his word. Only God knows the heart.

But in the case of infants, not even an oral, conscious confession is available. Saarnivaara writes:

> The infant cannot, of course, have a conscious conviction of its sinfulness, neither can it have a conscious experience of the grace and salvation of God in Christ. It cannot consciously trust in Christ and surrender to him. Its faith must be an unconscious faith, for Christ says that an infant can receive the kingdom of God, that is, have faith.[1]

Christ used infants and small children as examples of how adults must become to enter God's kingdom. From that it is clear that infants and small children *receive the gift of God's grace freely whenever it is offered to them. When a child is baptized,* adults need only rest on the promise of the cleansing from sin that comes through baptism. They can be confident that *infants will receive such cleansing freely.* For it is to such as these that the kingdom of heaven belongs. In baptism the Spirit works faith in the unconscious infant or small child. With the older child there must be an oral confession before baptism to attest to the faith. In the baby this faith is created *through* baptism. Infants and small children are examples of how to receive faith and the kingdom.

Saarnivaara writes:

> The meaning of baptism, however, is that *the baptized person should consciously repent, experience salvation in Christ, and give his life to Him.* When a person is baptized in infancy, these things must come to pass in his life after he has reached the age of discretion, just as in the Old Covenant those circumcised in their infancy had to have a conscious circumcision of their heart later, to love God above all things, to trust in Him, and obey Him.[2]

While faith and rational thought are not the same, Scripture does require that children be brought up in the faith (Ephesians 6:4). As a child grows more aware of things, the faith that baptism creates may not mature with the child. A child needs to be brought up "in the nurture and admonition of the Lord." Children need to be helped to see the blessings of their baptism.[3] Thus, the infant's baptismal faith must become a *conscious* faith.

The infants of Christian parents are *all* to be baptized, for such receive the kingdom of heaven and the gift of faith. Baptism is the "means of grace" by which infants' sins are washed away. Infants are "brought to Jesus" in the waters of baptism (Matthew 19:13-15; Mark 10:13-16; Luke 18:15-17). Galatians 3:27 promises that in baptism infants and small children "put on Christ."[4] Again, adults can truly rejoice in the gift of baptism. They can be *absolutely* certain of their child's salvation in the waters of baptism. Such is the gift and promise of God!

The proper sequence of events

Is there a certain order to be followed when one comes to the faith? And what is that order? With adults, the gospel is first proclaimed. Then faith follows. And last of all, the new convert is baptized. But the sequence is not the same in infant baptism.

Texts such as Acts 22:16, John 3:5, Ephesians 5:26, and Titus 3:5 all speak of an order. The gospel is shared. Then comes belief. Last is baptism. The order makes sense with adults. But that order cannot be used as reason against infant baptism. That assumes that the person baptized must be able to explain his faith. It assumes a certain degree of rational thought. But must God's Word be articulated and rationally understood for a person to be saved?

Where is that notion in Mark 10 with Jesus and the little children? Rather, Mark 10 and the little children shows that we *can* bring infants to Jesus. Rational thought just never was the issue for the little ones.[5] God works in a different way with children. Rather than having to win over their rational thinking, God has *less* to do in creating infant faith. While adults and older children need to think through things in the hearing of the Word, that is just not so with the infant.

Cullman explains the relation and order between faith and baptism:

> The New Testament relation between faith and Baptism does not so unambiguously and indisputably affirm that faith leads to Baptism. This is, of course, true of the cases recounted in the New Testament of adult heathens and Jews. But for those other Baptisms mentioned, this sequence of events does not hold good. On the contrary, in them Baptism leads to faith, and this contrary order applies to all: baptism is the starting point of faith. What applies to all must be regarded fundamental. In the class of individual adults who come over from Judaism or heathenism, we deal with a reverse operation: faith

brings them to Baptism, and Baptism, by which they are received into the community of Christ, leads them to faith. . . .[6]

Cullman parallels baptism to the miracles of Christ. In Christ's healing works, the faith of the healed person was not the most basic or decisive factor. The healed man in John 5 would be a good case in point. The man never responded to Jesus' desire to save his soul. Instead, he reported Jesus to "the Jews." In many cases, the order, faith-leads-to-the-baptism/miracle, is reversed.[7] But both are part of the miracle of salvation.

Again, what a joy it is to parents to know that baptism creates saving faith in their little ones! God works in the little baby the grandest of all his miracles, the miracle of faith in Jesus Christ. This is the promise and assurance of God's Word, and a true comfort for parents!

The poor witness of many baptized as infants

Many of those baptized as infants do not stay in the church or live Christian lives. Some people see that as a problem with infant baptism. If infants are saved through baptism, why are there people who are such poor witnesses to what God did in their infant baptism? Underlying this objection is a certain sense of "once saved—always saved." In other words, if one is saved in one's infant baptism, the person should go to heaven when he or she dies. Once one becomes a Christian, the kingdom of heaven is supposedly guaranteed. Scripture takes issue with this idea though. Scripture teaches that true believers can and often do fall away from the faith:

Matthew 13:5-7,18,20-22: "Other seeds fell on rocky ground, where they had not much soil, and immediately they sprang up, since they had no depth of soil, but when the sun rose they were scorched; and since they had no root they withered away. Other seeds fell upon thorns, and the thorns grew up and choked them. . . . Hear then the parable of the sower. . . . As for what was sown on rocky ground, *this is he who hears the word and immediately receives it with joy*; yet he has no root in himself, but *endures for a while*, and when tribulation or persecution arises on account of the word, immediately he falls away. As for what was sown among thorns, this is he who hears the word, but the cares of the world and the delight in riches choke the word, and it proves unfruitful."

2 Peter 2:20-22: "*For if, after they have escaped the defilements of the world through the knowledge of our Lord and Savior Jesus Christ*, they are again entangled in them and overpowered, the last state has become worse for them than the first. For it would have been better for them never *to have known the way of righteousness* than *after knowing it* to turn back from the holy commandment delivered to them. It has happened to them according to the true proverb, The dog turns back to his own vomit, and the sow *is washed* only to wallow in the mire."

Hebrews 6:4-6: "For it is impossible to *restore again to repentance* those who have once been enlightened, *who have* tasted the heavenly gift, and have become partakers of the *Spirit, and* have tasted *the goodness of the word of God and the powers of the age to come*, if they then commit apostasy, since they crucify the Son of God on their own account and hold him up to contempt."

Hebrews 10:26f: "For if we sin deliberately *after receiving the knowledge of the truth, there no longer remains a sacrifice for sins*, but a fearful prospect of judgment, and a fury of fire which will consume *the adversaries.*"

While faith is not the same as conscious reason, the infant must still be brought up in the Lord. That way the infant's baptismal faith becomes a conscious faith. While an infant is saved in baptism he or she can still fall away from the grace given in baptism. So Scripture is clear on bringing children up in the faith of their baptisms:

Ephesians 6:4: "Fathers, do not provoke your children to anger, but bring them up in the discipline and instruction of the Lord."

Deuteronomy 6:7: ". . . and you shall teach them diligently to your children, and shall talk of them when you sit in your house, and when you walk by the way, and when you lie down, and when you rise."

Infants must later be *taught* the meaning of their baptism for their lives!

Romans 6:3-4f: "Do you not know that all of us who have been baptized into Christ Jesus were baptized into his death? We were buried therefore with him by baptism into death, so that as Christ was raised from the dead by the glory of the Father, we too might walk in the newness of life."

Paul reminds his readers of their baptisms! He explains that baptism is the basis for the new life in Christ. Sin should no longer live in the Christian's body. But his readers needed to be reminded of that! So too, children need to be reminded of what God has done in their baptisms. Children should be brought up in the Lord. When parents neglect their children's spiritual growth, they leave their children prone to fall away from their baptismal faith. Thus some infants become poor witnesses to their baptisms.

But let's go back for a moment! While infants can fall away when older if not brought up in the faith, keep in mind the positive. They're still falling away from a true and precious faith. That faith, at the least, served them in their infancy. Baptism insures the child in infancy of its salvation. Such is the wonderful promise of God! Indeed, "hinder them not!"

Infant blessing versus infant baptism

Instead of infant baptism, many churches practice what is called infant "blessing."[8] The custom goes back to Christ (Mark 10:13-16). After the people brought babies to Jesus, "he took them in his arms, laid his hands on them, and blessed them" (verse 16). But wait a minute! How can the same passage be used for both infant baptism and infant blessing? Actually, the passage shows that these "little ones," identified by Luke's Gospel as infants, *"believe."* When infants were brought to Christ, they received the kingdom of God. That doesn't mean right away the children were baptized. But whether Jesus baptized the children or blessed them is not the issue. The issue is how we *today* can bring our little ones to him. Are children to be brought to Jesus in infant baptism or in an infant blessing?

First, infant blessing *was never ordained* by the Lord. Baptism was. *Baptism* was given to the Church as a means of bringing people to the faith (Matthew 28:18-20).[9] Second, infant blessing does not have God's grace promised with it or the power of the Word as baptism does. Baptism is a "sacrament" while infant blessing simply is not. Baptism is a means of making infants holy.

Gottfried Hoffman, in an essay on infant faith, warns against the trend in churches today toward infant blessing. Churches are starting to invest in infant blessing what had been seen as given in baptism. But this is not a biblical trend. When Jesus laid his hands on the small children, he did not command the practice. The Lord just said that he wanted the small ones brought to him! He said nothing about blessing the children. In no way can infant blessing be seen as a substitute to the wonderful blessings of God given in water baptism![11] God's grace and kingdom are offered in baptism.[12] That means that one need only trust in the words of Jesus. Those little ones so brought to him will be granted faith.

But people still get stuck on the fact that Jesus did not baptize the little ones. *Jesus never baptized*! ". . . Jesus himself did not baptize, but only his disciples" (John 4:2). That Christ did not baptize these children but blessed them *should not be found surprising. Jesus never baptized adults either*! Mark 10:13-16 does not in any way detract from infant baptism.

Oscar Cullman and Joachim Jeremias, two modern scholars, have noted a common usage of the word "to forbid, hinder, prevent." The word is used in Mark 10:14; Matthew 19:14; and Luke 18:16. These texts refer to the children brought to Christ and his blessing of them. We are not to hinder or keep the infant from Jesus. But the word is also used in other passages that *refer to baptism*!

"To hinder, prevent, forbid" is used in Acts 8:36; 10:47; 11:17 and Matthew 3:13. The word also occurs in the early Christian "Gospel of the Ebionites" (Epihanias 30:13). Regularly, this verb "prevent" (*koluein*) crops up in texts treating baptism. "Who can prevent this person's baptism?" This question thus must have been a standard question in a first century baptism. By using this term with baptisms, Luke points toward the early

49

rites of baptism.[13]

After Philip taught the eunuch (Acts 8:30f), the eunuch asked Philip: "Here is water. What keeps me from being baptized?" (Acts 3:36) The eunuch must have been taught the meaning *and custom* of baptism by Philip prior to coming upon the body of water. Why else would the eunuch say, "What *keeps* me from being baptized?" A much more direct request would have been "Can I be baptized?" or "Will you baptize me?" As part of an early baptismal rite, the question would then make sense.

Acts 10:47 says: "Can anyone *forbid* water?" "Water" is used in a figure of speech called "personification." Can water be forbidden? The question itself seems strange. But it makes sense if it were part of an early baptismal rite. The one bringing the person to baptism would address this question to the one baptizing. The one baptizing could then accept or decline the request made for the person. A reason would have to be given to refuse the baptism.[14]

In Acts 11:17, the strange phrase is again found with the baptism of Cornelius's family: "Who was I—could I *stop* God?"[15]

Matthew 3:14 and the Gospel of the Ebionites use the word "hinder" in the same way as in Acts 11:17. These two cases are in the context, again, of baptism!

After all these texts on baptism, we then come to Mark 10:13-14 and the account of the little children and Christ. Cullman notes the parallels to the texts on baptism (especially Acts 10:47; 11:17).[16] There are:

1. The one to be blessed.
2. The one who requests the blessing.
3. The one who wishes to reject the request.
4. The one who carries out the blessing.
5. The phrase "forbid them not."

Cullman thus sees more than a mere blessing of the

little children. The texts use a word that was used with baptism. By using the word "hinder" the Gospel writers are trying to lead the reader to see Jesus' blessing of the children in terms of baptism! When the question of infants and their baptism came up, one would then have to say "forbid them not."

This was also how the early church used the phrase. Jeremias writes:

> . . . the words of Jesus, "Let the children come to me, and do not forbid them" (Matthew 19:14), were generally understood as an injunction to let the children be baptized, and even Tertullian, although in *De Baptismo* 18 he opposes a too early age for baptism, does not. . . try to escape from this interpretation of the passage as applying to baptism. Similarly the *Apostolic Constitution* base their claim that the young children (nepia) should be baptized on the words "Forbid them not." The application of the passage about the blessing of children to baptism . . . must be considerably older [than the end of the second century.][17]

Jeremias compared the Greek of John 3:5; Mark 10:15; Luke 18:17; and Matthew 18:3 to Justin Martyr's *Apology* I 61.4 and *Const. Apost.* VI 15.5, two early Christian texts. He concluded that from early on these passages were seen in terms of baptism. Jeremias found over four sets of wording in these Scripture texts that are paralleled in the early Church fathers.[18,19]

Before Jewish converts were circumcised or baptized, they were asked about their motives. Was there thus a "hindrance" to their entry into Judaism? The Jews were asking this question with *their* baptism long *before* Christian baptism. The church would just have taken over the Jewish rites at this point.[20]

But there is a further parallel to baptism in the blessing texts. The laying on of hands was a normal part of the early rite of baptism. The early Christians were used to seeing a good number of baptisms. In Jesus' blessing of the children, he laid his hands on them. Wouldn't baptism have come to mind when the early Christian read of Jesus and the children?[21] There is good reason, then, to see Jesus' blessing the children as speaking also to infant baptism.

5.

CHRIST'S COMMAND IN MATTHEW 28:18-20

"Andrew, show me just one place in the Scripture where Jesus says, 'Baptize babies.' " That's all she asked for. That was all my friend in college said she needed to believe in infant baptism.

Promptly, I replied with Christ's words in Matthew 28:18 to baptize all nations. But that did not satisfy her. The very next phrase goes on and says that they all are to be taught. How can one teach a baby? Surely this shows that Christ's words were really meant for those who were older who could understand and so be taught. It wasn't long before I came to see that this was a hang-up for a lot of people. If Jesus had wanted infants baptized, why didn't he ever just simply say so?

The Swiss Karl Barth, who is thought by many people to be the greatest theologian of this century, once bluntly said: ". . . nowhere in the New Testament is infant baptism either permitted or commanded."[1] Of course, it doesn't take a Karl Barth to say that. There is a growing consensus among Christians that infant baptism boils down to a mere church custom. God never said "baptize babies." Where in the Bible does it say *that*?

Many Christians who believe in the baptizing of babies get stumped trying to find just such a passage. Admittedly, nowhere in Scripture can one find the words "Baptize babies." But does that mean that the church has no business baptizing these little ones? To take the matter a little further, we might ask: why baptize at all?

An overview of the Gospel of Matthew

Probably one of the first passages to come to mind would be Jesus' command in the last chapter of Matthew. The familiar words read: "Go therefore and make disciples of all nations, baptizing them in the name of the Father and of the Son and of the Holy Spirit, teaching them to observe all that I have commanded you." But to fully appreciate these words, we need to go back and review Matthew's Gospel as a whole.

From the start, Matthew is intensely Jewish. Already in the first chapter, this Jewish orientation is clear. Matthew opens his Gospel with a genealogy of Christ. But unlike Luke's genealogy which begins with Adam, Matthew starts with Abraham, the father of Israel. From Abraham Matthew traces the lineage of Christ through Isaac, Jacob, Judah, David, and the kings of Israel. Matthew's genealogy traces the whole of Israel's history. First and foremost, Jesus is the promised Messiah of *Israel* who died for the world. For it is from *the Jews* that the Messiah comes!

Matthew begins with the words "the book of the genealogy . . . ." These words echo Genesis 2:4 and 5:1: "These are the generations." (Some translations render the phrase, "This is the account [or history] . . . ." The book of Genesis is divided into ten such sections, each beginning with the same phrase.) Even as Genesis began the story of the people of the Messiah, so Matthew begins the story of the Messiah himself. And for Matthew, Christ

is both the "Son of David" and the "Son of Abraham." As
the Son of David he stands in the kingly line from King
David. He is truly then the "King of the Jews" (Matthew
27:11). As the Son of Abraham he is the One who fulfills
the hopes of Israel that began with God's promises to
Abraham. So the genealogy in Matthew 1 traces the people of the promise from Abraham through the nation of
Israel to the Lord Jesus himself.

Matthew 1 concludes with the appearance of an angel
to Joseph (verses 18-25). In the Old Testament an angel
announced the birth of the mighty Samson. An angel visited his father and mother. Samson would "save" his people from the Philistines. How significant it would be from
a Jewish point of view to see an angel now visiting
Joseph. The angel tells Joseph that Jesus would fulfill the
words of the Prophet Isaiah, one of the greatest of Israel's
prophets. So Jesus will save "his people" from their sins.
From the very first chapter, Matthew tells of the One who
would save the Jews from their sins. Thus Matthew is
written from an intensely Jewish perspective.

At the same time Matthew is utterly Jewish, the
Gospel is also an indictment against the Jews. From the
very beginning, the Jewish leaders oppose Jesus. In
Matthew 9:3, the Jewish leaders already accuse Jesus of
blasphemy. Jesus' parable of the wicked tenants is direct-
ed especially against them. Over and over again, Jesus
refutes the Pharisees and teachers of the Law (12:1-3, 22-
37; 15:1-20; 23:1-39). The conflict reaches a peak when
Jesus is crucified for his supposed blasphemy.

But not only does the conflict lie with the Jewish leaders, the Jewish people themselves are equally guilty.
Jesus says in 8:10-13 that no one in Israel has such faith
as the Roman centurion. Jesus describes Israel in 11:16-
19 as a generation that is turning away. Later on he
calls Israel spiritually blind, deaf, and without understanding. Finally, it is the Jewish people who demand

the crucifixion (27:23). So H. N. Ridderbos can suggest: "One could say that the Gospel of Matthew is a single great apology for the Christian faith in the light of the Old Testament, and thus also a single great indictment of the Jews' unbelief."[2]

In the face of the Jews' lack of faith in their own promised Messiah, Matthew inserts the story of the Gentiles. While Jesus has come for the lost sheep of Israel, "he [Matthew] makes it increasingly clear that, to Israel's shame, it would be the Gentiles and not the Israelites who would inherit the promise (e.g., 2:11; 8:11,12; 15:27,28; 27:54)."[3] In Matthew 2:1, the Gentile Magi come to visit the baby Jesus. It is a Gentile centurion who is the example of faith to all Israel in 8:5. At the cross, another centurion recognizes the Christ. Gentiles were considered by the Jews as "non-people." Jesus uses the "non-people" as a witness to the Jews.

But it's not just the Gentile "non-people" who are Jesus' examples of faith. Keep in mind that other groups who were "non-people" from the Jewish perspective would also be saved by the Messiah. Many of the Gentiles that Matthew points out in Jesus' lineage turn out to be *women*. Jesus also came for tax collectors and sinners (Matthew 9:10-13). Jesus came for the lepers (8:1-3). He came for the possessed (8:28-34) and the sick (9:35). What a study in contrasts! As the chosen people reject their own Messiah, it is the "non-people" who then benefit from his salvation! Jesus receives these "non-people" as his chosen people (22:1-10).

Peter confesses Jesus as the Christ, the Son of the living God (16:16). Upon this confession, Jesus says he will build his church and give the keys of the kingdom of heaven (16:19). After Peter's confession in chapter 16, the Gospel of Matthew begins to gather momentum. The conflict rises. The crescendo builds. Tensions heighten as the climax draws near. With this confession, the journey to the cross outside Jerusalem begins.

Matthew 17 then relates the Transfiguration with Moses and Elijah, two Old Testament saints (17:3). Themes such as the church (16:18; 18:15-20), the kingdom of heaven (16:19; 18:16,23-35; 19:23-26; 20:1-16) and the saints of the Old Testament (17:1-13) dominate this section. And along the way are two chapters (18 and 19) devoted to infants and small children.[4] Jesus holds up the little ones as examples of faith to the Jews. One must become as a little child to enter into the kingdom of heaven. Then as Jesus enters Jerusalem (chapter 21:16), the small children are singing praises to Jesus. Jesus says: "Yes; have you never read, 'Out of the mouth of babes and sucklings thou hast brought perfect praise'?"

Matthew's Gospel reaches its peak in Christ's command to baptize all nations. No longer is salvation only of the Jews. Salvation has come to the "non-people," all nations—to the blind, the Gentiles, the women. And foremost among the people Matthew has highlighted along the way are the small children. All throughout the journey to the Matthew 28 mountaintop, the small children are held up as examples of the faith.

David Scaer lists seven points from Matthew holding up little children as examples:[5]

1. They are held up as those who receive the kingdom.
2. They are held up as examples of sanctification.
3. To receive the Christian child is to receive Christ, because Christ is living in the child.
4. A special warning and punishment of the millstone and being tossed into the sea are attached to those who offend the Christian child.
5. Jesus gives special instruction to those who by chance might possibly offend.
6. Children are identified as the lost whom Jesus

especially came to save in the parable of the lost sheep.
7. Matthew 19 has the famous words of Jesus to let the children come unto him.

Small children are important people too! So when the Gospel of Matthew reaches its climax with the command in Matthew 28, are not small children surely to be included? Scaer says: "It seems as if our Lord here with his many references to children was already aware of the problem that the church would have with children and their place in the kingdom of heaven."[6]

A close look at Matthew 28:18-20

In Matthew 28:18-20, Christ says: "Go therefore and make disciples of all nations [or, people], baptizing them in the name of the Father, and of the Son, and of the Holy Spirit, teaching them to observe all that I have commanded you."

"All nations" are to be made disciples. After reading Matthew's Gospel, Christ's words would clearly include the little children as well. Matthew says that disciples are made *by* baptizing and teaching. To make all nations disciples requires that they be baptized. Since the verb, "make disciples," is a command, so also is the whole sentence. That means that "baptizing" and "teaching" are *also* part of Jesus' command.[7]

Baptism is given very strong exclamations and emphasis. First, Matthew 28:18-20 is a clear command of the Lord to baptize. Second, he adds the word "nations" which is the Greek "ethnee," from which the English word "ethnic" comes. Christ's gospel is not to be limited to the Jews or a *particular group of people*. Jesus intended it for all nations, the whole world. Finally, Christ adds further emphasis with the word "all" (*panta*). ". . . *panta ta ethnee* [all nations] is to be interpreted without any restriction whatsoever."[8] In light of the carefully chosen and unusually strong words of Jesus, dare the church exclude any group of people (i.e. infants) from baptism?

Matthew 28:18-20 firmly commands the baptism of all nations. One might say that Matthew 28 is the "presumption" in the matter. In debate, presumption is defined as the "occupied ground." The job of the one who disagrees is to take over that "ground."[9] In other words, by setting forth Matthew 28:18-20 as a clear text for the baptism of all, the important ground is occupied. The "burden of proof" is shifted to those who wish to exclude a group of people from baptism. They must, with success, "take over" the ground occupied by Matthew 28:18-20. They must show why the Church should *not* baptize the little ones. Why should a group of people be denied baptism, given the Lord's clear words to baptize?

Matthew 28 says: "Make disciples by baptizing and teaching." But others say that this verse should read: "Having made disciples of, baptize and teach." That would split off "baptizing" and "teaching" from "make disciples." Baptizing would *follow* the making of a disciple. However in that case the original Greek phrasing would have been different.[10] The passage is simply not speaking of two successive activities, but of making disciples of all nations by baptizing and teaching. If infants and children are to be made his disciples, they too must be baptized.

But what of "teaching"? If infants are to be made disciples, how are they to be taught? First of all, the basis for this objection is not in Scripture but man's own reason. What then of the unborn John the Baptist's joy when the mother of Jesus visited (Luke 1:15,41,44)? Luke 1:15 shows that infants are *capable* of the things of faith. Adults should not inject *into* Scripture their own human notions of what infants can or cannot receive. The command to baptize is clear. The command to teach is also clear. Infants are baptized and then brought up in the teachings of the faith, thoroughly fulfilling what is involved in Christ's command to make disciples.[11]

The Old Testament and children

While children were important people in Matthew's Gospel, does that mean these are members of "all nations"? Consider the Old Testament judgments of nations. The following is a small sample:

> Exodus 11:5: "And all the firstborn in the land of Egypt shall die, from the first-born of Pharoah who sits upon his throne, even to the first-born of the maidservant who is behind the mill; and all the first-born of the cattle."

> 1 Samuel 15:3: "'Now go and smite Amalek, and utterly destroy all that they have; do not spare them; but kill both man and woman, infant and suckling, ox and sheep, camel and ass.'"

> Isaiah 13:16 (against Babylon): "Their infants will be dashed in pieces before their eyes . . . ."

> Isaiah 14:21: "Prepare slaughter for his sons because of the guilt of their fathers, lest they rise and possess the earth and fill the face of the world with cities."

> Isaiah 20:4 (against Egypt and Ethiopia): "So shall the king of Assyria lead away the Egyptians captives and the Ethiopia, both the young and the old, naked and barefoot, with their buttocks uncovered, to the shame of Egypt."

> Jeremiah 18:21 (against Judah): "Therefore deliver up their children to famine."

Jeremiah 38:23: "All your wives and your sons shall be led out to the Chaldeans."

Lamentations 2:11,19: "My eyes are spent with weeping; my soul is in tumult; my heart is poured out in grief because of the destruction of the daughter of my people, because infants and babies faint in the streets of the city. . . . Arise, cry out in the night, at the beginning of the watches! Pour out your heart like water before the presence of the Lord! Lift your hands to him for the lives of your children, who faint for hunger at the head of every street."

Ezekiel 9:6: "Slay old men outright, young men and maidens, little children and women . . . ."

Hosea 2:4 (against Israel): "Upon her children also I will have no pity, because they are children of harlotry."

Hosea 9:12-13: "Even if they bring up children, I will bereave them till none is left. Woe to them when I depart from them! Ephraim's sons, as I have seen, are destined for a prey; Ephraim must lead forth his sons to slaughter."

Joel 2:16 (against Judah): "Gather the people. Sanctify the congregation; assemble the elders; gather the children, even nursing infants."

Nahum 3:10 (against Nineveh): "Yet she was carried away, she went into captivity; her little ones were dashed into pieces at the head of every street . . . ."

> 2 Chronicles 20:13 (against Judah): "Meanwhile all the men of Judah stood before the Lord, with their little ones, their wives, and their children."

> Joshua 8:35 (against Israel): "There was not a word of all that Moses commanded which Joshua did not read before all the assembly of Israel, and the women, and the little ones, and the sojourners who lived among them."

> Nehemiah 12:43: "And they offered great sacrifices that day and rejoiced, for God had made them rejoice with great joy; the women and children also rejoiced. And the joy of Jerusalem was heard afar off."

Children were included in the judgment against Nineveh. In Jonah 3:5, the prophet preaches against Nineveh, and the people: ". . . put on sackcloth from the greatest of them to the least of them." The word for "least" can refer to even the youngest.[12] But further, the Hebrew *phrase* "greatest to the least" is *always* all-inclusive, no matter the age, class, or status.[13] The phrase occurs in Jeremiah 6:13: "For from the least to the greatest of them, every one is greedy for unjust gain." Jeremiah 31:34: ". . . they shall all know me, from the least of them to the greatest. . . ." Esther 1:5: ". . . the king gave for *all* the people . . ., both great and small." 1 Samuel 5:9: ". . . the hand of the Lord was against the city, . . . and he afflicted the men of the city, both young and old. . . ." Ronald Williams, an expert in Hebrew grammar, concurs that the phrase is emphatic and inclusive.[14] Jonah 4:11 speaks of "the 120,000 persons who do not know their right hand from their left." This is a sign of mental infancy. Children from birth to three years old are the chief members of this class.[15] That means *infants* were among the 120,000 Ninevites who faced judgment.

Exodus 20:5 explains why children and infants were judged with the nations: "For their fathers' sins I punish children." David Scaer writes: ". . . in the cursing and blessing of the nations, the children are without exception included."[16] "All nations" would thus entail infants to Jesus' listeners.

Actually, the inclusion of the little ones in the cursing of the nations leaves things on a rather somber note. What parent could read the Old Testament cursing of the infants of nations without a deepfelt pain. It could even seem unjust. But children are not innocent of sin. Nor are any of us! We are *all* a "non-people," guilty, falling short of God's glory and lost in our sins.

Why else would Jesus have so strongly emphasized his command to baptize? Jesus wanted to impress upon his people that *all* nations be baptized. This is not an "eleventh commandment." Baptism is an expression of God's undeserved love for us. And we all need that grace of God that comes to us in baptism, especially our little ones! Jesus does not want *anyone* to perish. And that means the small child, the baby. Jesus' concern that the whole world be baptized, even the least, flowed out of his desire that every lost sinner be saved, a desire that took him to the cross on Calvary.

What a sweet comfort for parents to be able to bring their infant to baptism! They can have the absolute certainty of their child's being made a disciple of the Lord Jesus. When Jesus says, "Let the children come to me," they can rejoice as the Lord takes *their* little ones into his loving arms, as he embraces them in the waters of Holy Baptism. And as the small child is baptized, our Lord reminds the parents of the grace *they* received in their baptism, his love for them, his love for the whole world in his death on the cross.

6.

PAUL'S COMPARISON OF CIRCUMCISION AND BAPTISM

A woman asked her non-Christian friend to come and visit her church. Eventually, the man gave in to her earnest request. He even took his little boy along. During the sermon the pastor asked if the people would be willing to have a plain, large seal put upon their foreheads. When people saw the seal, they would then know that the person was a Christian. In the car on the way home, the boy asked his dad what a Christian was. The father tried to explain as best he could. The little boy leaned over to look at his dad's forehead: "Daddy, are you a Christian?" . . .

The seal on the forehead signified the person's faith and membership in God's special family. In the middle ages many important families had a "coat of arms," a symbol of their family that they might display on a shield. Other families had a family seal on a ring that could be printed onto letters. These markers identified family members to others.

The seal of circumcision

The people of Israel also used a seal. They would circumcise their men and boys. While the Christian church does not circumcise, the church has a seal as well—water baptism. And in many ways circumcision and water baptism are very much alike.

But what are circumcision and baptism seals of? What do they picture? What do they represent? Many people think that circumcision was a sign of one's membership in the nation of Israel. Circumcision kept the Jews distinct as a people. But there is more to circumcision than that. And that wasn't even its purpose to begin with. Circumcision did not begin with Moses but with *Abraham*, in God's covenant with the patriarch.[1] Other nations descended from Abraham also circumcised. The rite, then, was not for mere national identity.

At the same time, circumcision still marked a special people. God gave circumcision to Abraham on the basis of his *faith*. Paul explains in Romans 4:11: "He [Abraham] received circumcision as a sign or seal of the righteousness which he had by faith while he was still uncircumcised." In Romans 4:13-25, Paul tells how Abraham was counted righteous in Genesis 17 because of his faith in God. Verses 24 and 25 show that this faith was fulfilled in Jesus Christ. God instituted circumcision in relation to true, saving faith.

So Abraham became a father of faith to the Jewish people. They were a special people only because God chose them as his own. Circumcision was the seal of God's choice. But the seal was of no personal value without faith. If the people did not remain in a proper relationship with God, they would not enjoy his blessings. It is easy to see, then, why the Old Testament always speaks of faith as also necessary along with the rite.

Moses explained that a circumcision of the heart was required (Deuteronomy 10:16). In Deuteronomy 30:6 Moses promised: "And the Lord your God will circumcise your heart and the heart of your offspring, so that you will love the Lord your God with all your heart and with all your soul, that you may live." Leviticus 26:40-42 speaks of circumcision as a sign of repentance. Jeremiah, likewise, saw the "circumcision of the heart" as the true meaning and fulfillment of the physical rite. In Jeremiah 4:4, the prophet says: "Circumcise yourselves to the Lord, remove the foreskin of your hearts . . . ." Later, in 9:26 he says: ". . . for all these nations are uncircumcised, and all the house of Israel is uncircumcised in heart." Thus, circumcision must be accompanied by faith to be of any benefit before the Lord.

The Apostle Paul concurs in Romans 2:28,29 that the true Jew is one who is circumcised also in the heart, that is, by faith. In Philippians 3:3, Paul says that those who worship by the Spirit and rejoice in Jesus Christ are the truly circumcised. Circumcision goes hand in hand with faith. Circumcision without faith is therefore, for the individual, of no spiritual value. With faith, it is the fulfillment of the Old Testament covenant God made with Abraham, a covenant later fulfilled in the Messiah and salvation from sin.

As a seal or sign of faith, circumcision pointed toward an "objective" reality. Paul argues in Romans 3:1-4, "What if some were unfaithful? Does their faithlessness nullify the faithfulness of God? By no means!" Even without faith, the circumcision itself was still valid before God. Circumcision was a seal of God's promise. So Christ's coming as the Savior of Israel fulfilled the covenant. God's covenant and his faithfulness to it was an unchanging, "objective" reality. But that doesn't guarantee that people will benefit from his grace. Only by faith could men enjoy the actual, personal blessings of the covenant to which their circumcision attested.[2]

While circumcision was a sign of the faith Abraham had *before* circumcision, was that to be the norm for this seal and mark? First one was to come to faith and then be circumcised? No! The infants of his household and his descendants were to be circumcised as well (Genesis 17:9-14; Leviticus 12:3). From then on, the infants were to be circumcised on their eighth day. While explaining that circumcision must be accompanied by faith, Paul never criticized infant circumcision.

Parallels to baptism

Exploring circumcision is important to more fully appreciate the parallels to baptism. Baptism points to the "objective" reality of God's grace in Christ. But baptism's blessings are also appropriated by faith (Mark 16:16). Baptism and faith go hand in hand.[3] True faith leads to baptism just as through baptism God creates faith in the child's heart. In all these ways, baptism parallels circumcision.

Circumcision and baptism are very much alike even in the terms that Scripture uses for them. The New Testament uses the Greek word "*sphragizesthai*" (to seal) with baptism. Yet circumcision is called a "*sphragis*" (seal).[4] The circumcised are said to be "born again" and "holy." But the same is said of those who are baptized.[5]

Even the recipients of circumcision were the same as those baptized. Adults who wanted to become Jews were circumcised, as well as Jewish infants. While the adults were taught first the meaning of the faith before the rite, not so the Jewish infants. But isn't this the same distinction that applies to Christian baptism?[6] So if infants were circumcised, given the analogy, shouldn't they be baptized?

But wait a minute! Women were not circumcised. However, keep in mind that in the times before Christ the Jews baptized. And they baptized women. This was an added rite of cleansing for converts before the Passover. Women were included in Jewish baptism. In this sense then, Christian baptism supersedes *also* Jewish convert baptism.[7] But further, Galatians 3:28 and Acts 2:17,18 explain why New Testament baptism includes women. For in baptism, there is no longer male and female. God's saving work is for *all*.

The seed, the Messiah, was to be born of a woman (Genesis 3:15; Galatians 4:4). The seed was also to be a male (Galatians 3:16; Isaiah 7:14; 9:6). Salvation was to come to *both men and women* through the divinely ordained *male* seed. He would be the son of Abraham and the Son of God. That the sign before Christ should be limited to men is apt, even as the sign after Christ should be for all.[8]

Paul writes in Colossians 2:11-13: "In him also you were circumcised with a circumcision made without hands, by putting off the body of flesh in the circumcision of Christ; and you were buried with him in baptism, in which you were also raised with him through faith in the working of God, who raised him from the dead. And you, who were dead in trespasses and the uncircumcision of your flesh, God made alive together with him, having forgiven us all our trespasses."

So what does this mean? In Colossians 2:11, Paul speaks of "the circumcision of Christ" that is done not by human hands but by the putting away of the sinful body. Paul identifies this "circumcision of Christ" as baptism in verse 12. He says that in baptism Christians are buried with Christ and raised with him "through faith produced by the power of God." Paul continues further on this theme of true circumcision in verse 13. Verses 11 and 13 create a "sandwich effect" with verse 12. Paul discusses in verses 11 and 13 the true circumcision that puts away our sinful body. In verse 12 he calls that circumcision *baptism* where we are buried and raised with Christ.

Baptism is not a mere ritual or symbolic washing (Titus 3:5). In Colossians 2:11, Paul condemns the legalistic ritualism that the Jews made of circumcision.[9] At the same time, while making a direct analogy with baptism, Paul also shows how baptism differs from circumcision. While circumcision pointed *forward* to Christ's future work, water baptism points *back* to Christ's finished work. Baptism is given in connection with the grace from Christ's saving work. *In baptism*, we are buried and raised with Christ. Baptism, thus, takes us *into* Christ's historic, saving work.

In Colossians 2:11-13, Paul *directly* calls baptism the circumcision of Christ. In so doing, Paul makes an analogy between circumcision and baptism. Infants were circumcised by God's decree before they were old enough to be accountable for their Jewish faith. Thus they became partakers of the promise God gave to Abraham. If baptism is the circumcision of Christ, infants must also be baptized, even as they were circumcised. Galatians 3:27 says that "for as many of you as were baptized into Christ have put on Christ." In the next verses, the text says, "And if you are Christ's, then you are Abraham's offspring, heirs according to promise." By baptism infants become members of Christ, heirs of the promise, as did Old Testament infants by circumcision. For in baptism infants are "circumcised into Christ."

Cornelius was *baptized after* coming to faith. Abraham was *circumcised after* coming to faith. So baptism is the circumcision of Christ. That adults came to faith before circumcision in the Old Testament *did not annul the fact that infants were to be circumcised* on the eighth day. The full blessings of the rite would come later. Many of the circumcised infants never received the blessings of their circumcision when older since their hearts were never circumcised. *But the infants were still included in the rite.*

Further, circumcision was *primarily* performed on infants. After Abraham, that became the norm. Would not any mention of circumcision right away bring to mind *infants*? Isn't circumcision associated first with infants in the Jewish mind, or even ours today? So when Paul calls baptism the circumcision of Christ, wouldn't the early Christian naturally conclude infant baptism from infant circumcision? Why doesn't Paul somewhere explain these remarks if infant baptism is wrong? Especially since circumcision would evoke such images to an early Christian mind. "Circumcision" is practically synonymous with infants. So, given the background of "circumcision," to say infant baptism is not meant in Colossians 2 is to take the passage *out of context*! Indeed, the baptism of Jewish converts before Christ included infants, in the thinking of the day, *on the basis of* the circumcision of infants.[10]

To leave infants uncircumcised was considered a grave sin. Joshua 5:4-7 records: "And this is the reason why Joshua circumcised them: all the males of the people who came out of Egypt, all the men of war, had died on the way in the wilderness after they had come out of Egypt. Though all the people who came out had been circumcised, yet all the people that were born on the way in the wilderness after they had come out of Egypt had not been circumcised. For the people of Israel walked forty years in the wilderness, till all the nation, the men of war that came forth out of Egypt, perished, because they did not hearken to the voice of the Lord; to them the Lord swore that he would not let them see the land which the Lord had sworn to their fathers to give us, a land flowing with milk and honey. So it was their children, whom he raised up in their stead, that Joshua circumcised; for they were uncircumcised, because they had not been circumcised on the way."

Exodus 4:24-26 records: "At a lodging place on the way the Lord met him and sought to kill him [Moses]. Then Zipporah took a flint and cut off her son's foreskin, and touched Moses' feet with it, and he said, 'Surely you are a bridegroom of blood to me!' So he let him alone. Then it was that she said, 'You are a bridegroom of blood,' because of the circumcision."

The implications of this for infant baptism should be clear. The divine command to circumcise infants becomes equally the command to baptize infants today.

The reason our Lord commanded circumcision so strongly was that people were taking God's grace for granted. They were treating circumcision, a seal of faith given by God, with contempt. If the people of Israel took the sign of God's grace for granted, weren't they also showing their disregard for that saving grace itself?

Wouldn't our Lord want us, then, to take baptism seriously? To reject baptism is to reject the loving Father who gave this gift to his children. We should not abuse this gift. Neither baptism nor circumcision were ever part of God's Law, proper. They are expressions of his love. God gave man baptism as a seal of faith in Jesus Christ. Baptism thus shows that we are members of his special family. Shouldn't infants be given the seal that shows that they are part of God's family? After all, aren't they heirs to the promise in Christ as well?

7.

JEWISH BAPTISMAL CUSTOMS
AT THE TIME OF CHRIST

Every nation of the world has rules and procedures for those who wish to become citizens of the country. The laws vary from country to country. In some countries the process is very simple. In others it is more complex.

When Joe came to the United States, he decided he wanted to become a citizen. First, he had to apply for citizenship. Then Joe had to declare himself a "landed immigrant." Of course, there are factors that could prevent a "landed immigrant" status. A criminal or "undesirable" person would not be allowed. Nor would people with beliefs contrary to the Constitution of the U.S. government. Joe had no problem with any of these criteria. During a period of five years, he took classes on U.S. government and citizenship. In the meanwhile, his "green card" allowed him to work in the U.S. Finally, after the five year period, Joe pledged allegiance to the U.S. flag. He was a U.S. citizen, at last.

Jewish baptism

Even at the time of Christ there was a proper procedure to become a member of Israel. Israel's procedure was a little different, though, from what one might normally expect. To become a member of Israel one also had to become a Jew. One had to convert! The Jews required three things of their potential citizens. First, the males had to be circumcised. Second, they had to offer sacrifice. Finally, they were *all* to be baptized! When men converted to Judaism, baptism washed away the uncleanness of paganism. Thus the non-Jews became a new people. They became Jews, and as Jews, God's people!

While the Law and the Prophets did not demand this custom, the practice of baptizing converts goes back well before Christ. After the last of the prophets, two schools arose in Judaism, the schools of Shammai and Hillel. These schools fought over the proper interpretation of the Law. The school of Shammai said that a convert could eat the Passover meal if circumcised and baptized on the night before.[1,2] Hillel would not allow this. The rabbis in these two schools passed their teachings down orally. In the centuries after Christ, the rabbis finally wrote the oral teachings down. So the "Babylonian Talmud," the "Gemara Babylon," and the "Jerusalem Mishna" came to be. Along with Maimonides, they testify of the baptism of converts as a practice from long before Christ.[3]

Some believe that the practice of convert baptism began *after* the time of Christ. But that's rather doubtful. The Jews hated the early Christians. And there was not even the slightest hint of controversy over this practice as would be expected if the practice were *later* than the time of Christ and his baptism. Why would the Jews take up *Christian* customs? But the *reverse* would be understandable.

One of the actual written documents from before Christ speaks of convert baptism. One of the writings, named after the sons of Jacob, "The Testament of Levi," states: "With harlots and adulteresses shall ye be joined, and the daughters of the Gentiles shall ye take to wife, purifying them with unlawful purifications; and your union shall be like Sodom and Gomorrah."[4]

A fragment from this writing was found, as well as from the "Testament of Naphtali." These fragments, written in Aramaic, date to, at the latest, the second century B.C.[5] The author opposes such a baptism since it allows for mixed marriages and the baptism is not Scriptural (thus, "unlawful purifications").[6] But the baptism itself was clearly already in existence.

Epictetus, in 109 A.D. at the age of sixty, writes: "But when he assumes the sentiments of one who has been *baptized* and circumcised, then he both really is and is called a Jew." Epictetus says that the baptism of converts was standard practice. Given his age and when he writes, the practice must then be quite ancient. Understandably, the scholarly consensus today is that Jewish baptism began well before Christ.[7]

This is not the only evidence for a Jewish baptism before Christ. Matthew tells of the Jews going to great lengths to win Jewish converts (23:15). That also entailed the baptism of these converts. When John the Baptist baptized, the Jews were not the least bit surprised. They had no problem at all with John's baptism in itself. Their only concern was with the authority behind it. Their query attests to the existence of a Jewish baptism *before* Christ!

Now what makes the Jews' baptism from before Christ so interesting is that they baptized infants along with parents! Jewish baptism was so common that a book could be filled with all their baptismal laws. Just as when one becomes a U.S. citizen with one's little children, so it was also with the Jews. The children and infants were also received into the faith. A boy's circumcision depended on whether he was born before or after the mother's baptism. A girl was considered the same as any other Jewish girl if brought into Judaism before three years of age. Baptism was the girls' means of admission into Judaism.

Later Jewish teachers confirm the baptism of infants. Rab Huna (A.D. 212-297) speaks of a court demanding an infant baptism. His pupil, Abba, also speaks of the practice. Raba (A.D. 299-352) speaks of infant convert baptism in relation to the mother's baptism. The oldest Jewish sources simply take infant convert baptism for granted.[8,9] And there's not a single dispute among the Jews over an infant being baptized along with its parents. Indeed, the parents would even be called "newly born babes" after their baptism.[10] Baptism was said to be their "birth" into Judaism.[11]

Christ and his apostles never attacked the Jews' practice of baptizing babies. While they threw out other practices that the Jews had added on to God's law, this one they left intact. With the Jews baptizing infants, surely Christ and his apostles would have made it clear that Christian baptism was not for infants, if such were actually the case. After all, if Christians were to baptize, as had the Jews before them, would not infants, then, be included? What else could the early Christian conclude? The message to the early Christian was quite clear. The baptism of Christ must include infants.

Just as the Gentile infant and its parents were cleansed of the uncleanness of paganism, so the Christian infant is cleansed from the uncleanness of sin. In the name of the Triune God, Christian baptism would cleanse in a way the Jews' baptism could not. Thus infants are born again and become part of God's family, his people. Baptism brings the infant into a greater kingdom, the kingdom of heaven.

Old Testament practices

One can't but wonder, though, how the Jews thought to baptize their converts. And why was the Church so quick to take over the practice? One must keep in mind that the Jews, and later the Christians, had precedent for their practice already in the Old Testament. God had prepared man for his Messiah, and for his baptism. Much of later doctrine and practice was already foreshadowed in the Old Testament.

The Jews already from the time of the Old Testament practiced forms of baptism. Hebrews 6:2 speaks of various "baptisms" (*baptismon*) that the Jews practiced. Hebrews 9:19 also refers to such washings. Although they were not quite the same as the later Christian baptism, these and other Old Testament washings included children. And they were "forms" (or "types") of the water baptism to come. Some of these Jewish washings consisted of bathing, throwing or sprinkling water or blood (Exodus 29:4,21; Leviticus 14:7-9; 16:14-19; Numbers 19:7, 13-21; Ezekiel 36:2). These washings acted as "gospel" for the people. In other words, by such washings the people could have their sins taken away.[12]

Leviticus 16:14-19 talks about the sprinkling of blood that took away "the uncleanness" and sins of the people. The uncleanness here includes all "the people of Israel." That would mean even the youngest. That sprinkling was, thus, for the sins of the children and infants as well. Leviticus 14:7-9 speaks of the cleansing from uncleanness for those with infectious skin diseases. This is symbolic, a "form," of the cleansing from the leprosy of the sin in the waters of baptism. If a child had such a disease, he would have to be cleansed. In Numbers 19:7,13-21 the washing is for anyone who touched a dead body. Here too the cleansing waters symbolize baptism's cleansing from spiritual death. The washing was a "form," a prophecy, of that to come. The law and washings in Numbers 19:7,13-21 and Leviticus 14:7-9 were for *anyone* who touched the dead or had such a disease, even toddlers and infants. Toddlers and infants are very inquisitive little people. Incidents like this would happen. And pious parents would then have had to clean their child of uncleanness by baptism. Little children would be included, when necessary, in these earlier forms of baptism.

Ezekiel 36:25 speaks of God sprinkling water on Israel to cleanse her from uncleanness. With this cleansing God promised to create a new heart and a new Spirit within his people. Such a baptism would include infants since Israel's infants were also unclean. They too needed to be part of the cleansing (see verses 12,13).

Since these older forms of baptism included infants, one can see why later Jewish customs before Christ of washing or sprinkling blood included infants. These washings acted as "forms" of the later baptism. In baptism, infants are cleansed by the washing of Christ from the uncleanness of their sinful flesh, spiritual leprosy.

The Lord included infants in yet another form of baptism in the Old Testament. God baptized infants of Israel along with their parents at the Red Sea. So Paul explains in 1 Corinthians 10:1,2: "I want you to know, brethren, that our fathers were *all* under the cloud, and *all* passed through the sea, and *all* were baptized into Moses in the cloud and in the sea." Paul keeps on using the word "all" through the next few verses. *All* Israel went through the Red Sea with Moses and so were saved from death at the hands of the Egyptians. Paul says that the saving power of baptism was already foreshadowed in the events of the Red Sea. However, of special interest for our study, infants were numbered with their parents in the Red Sea. Note Paul's repeated and emphatic use of the word "all" in the passage. Paul explains that this incident was a form of the water baptism yet to come with Christ. Since infants were baptized in the cloud and in the sea and so united with Moses, so Christian baptism is given to infants that they may be united with Christ.

People need a frame of reference in the midst of change. The Old Testament washings and the washings of the Jews before Christ prepared them for the coming of the Lord. These baptismal forms even help us to understand water baptism. They highlight the saving work of God. And God's saving work is for all. Infants and small children have *always* been prime members of God's family.

8.

THE BAPTISM OF ENTIRE FAMILIES AND HOUSEHOLDS

A pastor at a local ministerial meeting got in a conversation with the minister of a nearby church. A family that had moved into the town had visited both their churches. The family eventually joined the pastor's.

"We baptized their children last Sunday."

"The baby too?" asked the minister.

"Sure," replied the pastor. "Our church believes in baptizing babies."

"I know, but it'd be a lot easier for me to swallow if the Bible gave us an example of it."

"But it does," shot back the pastor. "What about when whole households were baptized in Acts?"

"Like I said, just one example of a *baby* being baptized . . . ."

Recognizing a familiar impasse, the two men quickly moved on to a less controversial topic.

Along the same lines, the story is told of a man who in a dream found himself on Judgment Day on the wrong side of the Judge. He only realized the gravity of his situation when he saw his beloved children next to him. He pleaded that the Judge would spare at least the children though he himself could not hope for as much. He was told that the time for such concern had already been granted. That time had now passed. When the man woke up, while he realized it was only a dream, he and his family were baptized within the week.

New Testament households

The New Testament speaks of "whole households" being baptized. What comes to mind with the word "household" or "family"? Today one might think of a father, a mother, and perhaps one or two or children. A modern household can be fairly small in size. The probability of there being an infant in any particular household could be rather slight.

But a "household" or "family" to an ancient Jew, Greek, or Roman included the children and infants. Among the Romans, a family was defined as all those under the authority of the head of household. This could include the wife, sons (whether by birth or adoption), unmarried daughters, and the sons' families. No matter how long the line of living male descent, the group was considered a single family. The head of the household was called the *"pater familias."*[1,2] These households could become fairly large. But that was never considered a problem.

As a matter of fact, the Roman household even included the slaves and their children as well![3] Indeed, the Romans often judged wealth by the number of slaves:

> The very poor plebians are, of course, slaveless and servantless, and plenty of small tradesmen or minor officials get along with only two or three slaves-of-all-work; but it is impossible to be a "somebody" and exist in Rome without *at least ten slaves*. The social ladder and the size of the

familia ascend together until we find senators and the very rich equites who boast many more than two hundred in their city houses alone. "How many slaves has he got?" is the regular formula for asking "What's his fortune?"[4]

Households were clearly much larger than one might at first think. That means that there's a good chance that children and infants would be in a given "household" at a certain point in time. And in the household baptisms described in the book of Acts, the families baptized were *Roman.*

What about the Greek conception of a family? After all, the New Testament uses the Greek word for "*household*": "*oikos.*" In the earlier Classical period of Greek language and culture, the term "*oikos*" (household) included children and infants. Joachim Jeremias is probably the most renowned defender of infant baptism in recent times. He once wrote this in reply to his critic, Kurt Aland:

> . . . in Hesiod, Pindar, Plato and the tragic poets examples are found which become more numerous in the ensuing period. These show unambiguously that *oikos* denotes the family including the children; and the papyri confirm this range of meaning by the fact that *oikos* alternates with *panoikei* and *panoikia.* On the other hand I have not found in secular Greek usage any examples of *oikos* referring to "adults exclusively."[5]

The word "panoikia" is a more intense way of saying "household." The emphasis is on the *whole* household. Jeremias concludes: " . . . nowhere in the whole of Hellenistic Greek literature nor in the Jewish literature is *oikos* restricted to the adult members of the family."[6]

81

The phrase always includes the youngest members of the family.

The usage of "*oikos*" in the Greek Old Testament Scriptures also confirms this. Households, in the biblical sense, include children and infants. Jeremias found the phrase "he and his (whole) house" throughout the Old Testament. This "*oikos*" formula, when used, seems to have special reference to the infants and the youngest.[7]

We find an example of this in 1 Samuel 22:16-19. There Saul said to the priest Abimelech, "You must die, you and your *family (oikos)*." Verse 19 goes on to describe the judgment being carried out against the family: "And with the sword he also killed the people of Nob, the city of the priests, men and women, *children and infants*, cows, donkeys, and sheep." In this instance, the "family" included the infants. Verse 20 then makes it a point to record that only one of Abimelech's children escaped.

In 1 Samuel 1:21, we read: "The man Elkanah went up again with all his family (*oikos*) to make the annual sacrifice to the Lord and to pay his vow." The text right away adds in verse 22: "But Hannah didn't go. 'I'll wait till the boy is weaned,' she told her husband. 'Then I'll take him to appear before the Lord, and he will stay there always.' " Again, the author makes it a point to explain why the unweaned child and his mother did not go with the family.

Genesis 17:23 tells how everyone in Abraham's *household (oikogeneis)* was to be circumcised, even the infants: "Abraham took his son Ishmael and everyone he had bought, every male in his household, and circumcised their foreskin as God had told him." Earlier, verse 12 said that even infants eight days old were to be circumcised.

From such examples, it's clear that the use of "household" (*oikos*) in the Greek Old Testament clearly included infants and children.

This makes the use of "oikos" in the Acts household baptisms very important for doctrine. People like to point out that there were no infants singled out in the New Testament household baptism passages. Suppose there were no infants in any of these homes. Does that weaken the case for baptizing the whole household? As long as the writer uses the word "household" (*oikos*), the *whole* household would be included. This term, when left unqualified, includes everyone. Thus baptism is for *everyone* in the household. The mere use of this word in itself to describe the events shows that baptism is for even the infant.

Old Testament households

In the actual Hebrew Old Testament, the word for "household" is "*bayit.*" "*Oikos*" is its Greek translation. Jeremias explains that if the simple form, "house of such and such," is taken out, the vast majority of the phrases where "*bayit*" occurs would be in the phrase "he and his house." The Hebrew way of thinking and speaking emphasizes the father as the head of the family.[8]

After studying the *bayit* phrases, Jeremias concludes:

> *What group of people does the phrase "he and his house" have in view*? That is the vital question. The answer is as follows. In the Old Testament it denotes the *complete family* and in many cases the inclusiveness is emphasized with the addition of *kol.*[9]

The father eats his meal with his family (Deuteronomy 12:7; 14:2; 15:20; Numbers 18:31). The father changes dwelling places and takes all his family with him (Genesis 36:6; Exodus 1:1; 2 Samuel 2:3; 15:16). The father and his household seek refuge (Genesis 7:1; 1 Samuel 27:3), are stricken by plagues (Genesis 12:17), are annihilated (Genesis 34:30; Judges 18:25; Esther 4:14), and are burned (Judges 14:15) as a family unit, including the children and infants. The family offers sacrifice together (1 Samuel 1:21). All the males are circumcised (Genesis 17:23). The *entire* family serves the Lord (Joshua 24:15). In Genesis 45:18, Pharaoh ordered Joseph: "Take your father and your *families (bayit)*, and come to me, and I will give you the good of the land of Egypt; then live off the fat of the land." Verse 19 points out children as part of the family: "Take wagons with you from Egypt *for your children* and your wives." In Genesis 46:6,7 it is written: "And so Jacob and all his family came to Egypt. He took with him to Egypt his sons, his grandsons, his daughters, his granddaughters—all his offspring."

The Hebrew "*bayit*" and the Greek "*oikos*" were used throughout the intertestamental period for *entire* households, which included children and infants.[10] But "*oikos*" is the same word used by the New Testament writers. This word, as a rule, included infants and children. By using "*oikos*" without any further qualification, the writers show that infants were also to be baptized as members of a household. Whether or not the households had infants in actuality is beside the point. That "*oikos*" is used to describe the events shows that the full household is to be baptized. That would include infants. The language and terms used to describe the events demands the inclusion of infants.

Corporate personality

The ancient Jewish notion of "corporate personality" sheds further light on all this. In "corporate personality" the family acted as a single unit with the head of the household making decisions that were considered binding on all.

In Joshua 7, Achan disobeyed the Lord's command

and took some of the spoils of Jericho. Because of his actions "the Lord's anger burned against Israel." Achan's sin affected *all* of Israel. The whole nation was held responsible (verse 11). Achan was then identified as the sinner in Israel only after each of the families of Israel had come forward one by one (verse 14). Achan and his *entire family* were then stoned (verses 24,25).

In Numbers 16, Korah, Abiram, and Dathan spoke against Moses. The Lord then commanded the people to move away from the three men's tents. While the people moved away from the three tents, Dathan and Abiram came out with their families. Verse 27 records "little ones" in the families. As soon as Moses finished speaking to the people, the ground opened up and swallowed the families and all their property. The entire household was held responsible for the sin of its head.

In addition to the well known examples of Achan and Korah, there are other examples of this Old Testament concept of "corporate personality." In 2 Samuel 21:5ff seven of Saul's sons paid the penalty for Saul's sin. Exodus 20:5 explains that the sins of the fathers are visited upon their children. In today's society and its laws, the family is not viewed as the strong unit that it was with the Jews. Rights began for the Jew, not with the individual, but with the family unit.[11]

Jeremias argues from the point of view of Jewish "corporate personality" or "household unity":

> But when we consider family solidarity resting upon the authoritative influence of the head of the family it is scarcely conceivable that the baptism of a "household" did not include all its members. How much the corporate change of religion by a family was taken for granted can be seen from the regulation which was observed in certain Jewish Christian circles, that the unbaptized

members of the family must be excluded from the table-fellowship of the family; this regulation shows that the possibility that the children might not be baptized along with their parents was not contemplated at all. The way in which the solidarity of the family was taken for granted explains further why no reason was found for emphasizing or justifying especially the baptism of children.[12]

Very rarely were the circumcisions of the male infants pointed out when a group was circumcised. Their circumcision was simply the norm when the family/household entered into the faith. That was part of the "corporate personality" of the ancient Jewish family. This also explains in the "household" baptisms the fact that only the heads of households were pointed out. It was the faith of the *head* that was critical. Infant baptism followed simply as the norm.

Inclusiveness of baptism

In Acts 10:24, Cornelius assembled all his relatives and friends. According to Acts 10:2, he feared God with "all those in *his home (oikos)*." The "relatives" in Acts 10:24 thus would include his own family and children. Peter meets Cornelius and his family. Peter commands them all to be baptized (verse 48). Among Cornelius's relatives and friends, there would probably have been infants. In any case, they would have been baptized. *The text nowhere states that anyone was excluded from the baptism.*

The impact of verses 24 and 48, when viewed together, is that Cornelius, all his family and all his friends were baptized. More than likely, there was an infant sitting on some mother's lap. Acts 11:14 agrees with this interpretation by an angel's proclamation to Cornelius that "what he will tell you will save you and *everybody* in your home (*oikos*)." The language of 11:14 with "all" and

10:48 proves that if there were any infants in Cornelius'
household, Peter came to save them, too. They would
have been among those baptized and saved in Peter's
visit.

Oscar Cullman, a renowned New Testament scholar,
points out that the word "forbid" or "prevent" is used in
Acts 10. "Prevent them not" is also used with the
eunuch's baptism: "What prevents me from being baptized?" Yet while used with baptism here, the same
phrase is used of littlest children in Matthew and Luke—
thus with regard to the infants, "do not prevent" them
from being baptized, for of such is the kingdom of God.
The phrase here in Acts 10 just adds more reason to see
the text as mandating infant baptism.[13]

In Acts 16:15, Lydia and her household (*oikos*) were
baptized. Again, if any infants were in her family/house-
hold, they were baptized. R.C.H. Lenski, the well-known
Lutheran commentator, writes that the baptism of entire
households was the norm for the apostles:

> Where is the evidence that *oikos* ever meant less
> than "household," "family," referred only to the
> adults to the exclusion of the children? Granted
> that many servants and slaves were included, the
> likelihood of there being children is only increased;
> and who will count all the households thus received
> by baptism?[14]

But why were no infants singled out? Baird, a nine-
teenth century advocate of the doctrine, answers. It was
Lydia's faith that was decisive in the baptism of her
entire household:

> Of Lydia alone it is said that the Lord opened her
> heart; and upon this fact exclusively is predicated
> her baptism and that of her house. . . . If it be

insisted that they believed and therefore were baptized, we reply that had such been the conception of the sacred writer, it would have been easy and far more important for him to have stated their faith, as he has recorded their baptism. The supposition that they did in fact believe, only renders his silence on that point the more significant.[15]

In Acts 16:28-36 (especially 28,33), Paul and Silas visit the jailer's household (*oikos*) late at night. Would the hour preclude an infant's presence during Paul's visit? But who could say that the children and/or infants would be asleep at this time? Children and infants sleeping at midnight is a *cultural* bias that must not be read into the text.[16] If they were sleeping, they could have been awakened. They had just experienced an earthquake (verse 26)! And didn't the guests come to speak to the *entire* "household"? One cannot simply assume that the children and/or infants were asleep. The *whole* house was baptized.

Paul spoke the word to "everyone," to "all" that lived in the jailer's home (verse 33). In the prior verses (30 and 31), the concern is that *all* of the jailer's house/family be saved. Luke goes out of his way to show that *all* were part of these events! Thus, they *all* would have been baptized in verse 33. The hour of night and age are not even factors here. The strict, emphatic wording of this text shows that *everyone* in a household is to receive baptism. That would include infants!

Baird again comments on the decisiveness of the jailer's faith with regard to the household's baptism:

Here, again, we have a construction which remarkably ignores the question whether his house, as well as he, believed. It may be assumed that they were all of an age to hear and understand the gospel. It may be assumed that they, so understanding, believed also. But it may not be assumed that such knowledge and faith were the ground of their baptism, because the sacred writer puts it upon a different ground. It was as identified with him—as belonging to him, that they were included in the rite. "He was baptized,—he and all *his*; he and *none but* his; and they *because* they were his." Such is the force of the expression as it stands. In the same direction looks the closing expression. "He rejoiced with all his house,— he believing." . . . The statement which describes him alone, as believing, was an express and designed intimation that his personal faith was the controlling element in the case. . . . He was recognized and dealt with as the head of his house, precisely as was Abraham.[17]

The lack of mention of the other adults in the household is understandable. So also is the fact that infants were not singled out either. Because of the *jailer's* faith, his household was baptized.

In Acts 18:8, Crispus and *"all* who were in his home" believed and were baptized. The wording of the passage is, as usual, a very strict "all," with no exception made. In 1 Corinthians 1:16, Paul writes that he baptized the household of Stephanas. Only the faith of Stephanas, as the head of the household, is pointed out.[18] If either household had infants, they would have been among the baptized.

It comes as no surprise then that other individuals baptized were never singled out. The gospel was still spread, when possible, into the family as a unit. Even as Abraham's household was handled as a unit, so here. This custom from the Jews did not change. The Lord respects the order of the family.[19]

As review, in each of the passages examined *entire households* were baptized. "All" is repeated and emphasized in most of the cases. *No one*, then, was left out. Households among the Greeks, the Jews, and the Romans always included the infants. Even as Abraham believed as the head of the household, so his boys were circumcised. So even here, the role of the faith of the head of the family would be decisive with regard especially to the infants' baptisms. And more than likely, infants would have been included in one of the family baptisms. Uuras Saarnivaara concludes:

> In this historical context we see in a new light the fact that the Apostolic Church also baptized whole families, like those of Cornelius, the Philippian jailer, and Stephanas in Corinth. An unprejudiced mind would naturally suppose that the Church followed a practice similar to that customary among the Jews. . . . Isn't it something entirely unnatural to think that Christ and the Apostolic Church would have rejected infant baptism, commonly used then, without saying a word on the matter? Isn't it much more reasonable to think that infant baptism is not mentioned because it was regarded as something so natural, so much a matter of course, that it did not need to be mentioned? When whole families were baptized, everybody understood that the Church followed at this point the ways of the Synagogue.[20]

Infants are part of God's family too! When a parent brings a child to baptism, that parent becomes more than just a natural parent. The parent becomes also a spiritual parent to the child in bringing the child to the Lord. The Lord established and respects the family order. It is the Lord's will that the *whole* family be saved. Only by this can a family come to be everything that God would have it be. Only in Christ can the family unit be freed from the curse of sin. Only in Christ can there be a true recognition of parental authority and a true understanding of the roles of husband and wife. By saving a whole household, the Lord thereby creates the family of God. And infants are part of that family as well!

9.

MEMBERS, BY BAPTISM, OF THE FAMILY OF GOD!

What more can be said from the Scriptures? So far, we have seen that baptism saves from the effects of sin, that infants can believe and benefit from baptism. We saw whole households, which would include infants, being baptized. Christ commanded baptism for infants. Even the Jews' baptism included infants, which had its basis in the Old Testament washings. The analogy to circumcision, to the Red Sea, and more, have all shown the need for infants to be baptized. And in each case, we have seen how babies were made members of God's family of faith by baptism.

What more could be said? A lot! This idea of infants as members of God's family runs all through Scripture! As final words from the Scriptures, let's look at just a few of the other passages that show this.

The Gospels

Matthew 3:5,6 records: "Then went out to him Jerusalem and *all Judea and all the region about the Jordan,* and they were baptized by him in the river Jordan, confessing their sins" (see also Mark 1:5). A large number of people were coming to John the Baptist to be baptized. Surely infants were among those baptized. In this text, the Greek word "all" (*panta*) is used, the same word found in the Matthew 28 phrase "*all* nations" and in the Acts household baptisms. Without further explanation, that means "all" were baptized. And as we saw before, the Jews baptized the infants of converts.[1] Why didn't the Gospel writers record the exclusion of infants from John the Baptist's baptism if such had been the case?

Already with John the Baptist, baptism was the means to become a member of God's family. So it is not surprising that Jesus and later Paul were baptized (Matthew 3:16; Acts 9:18).

Their baptisms also help show that baptism is truly for *all*. But in contrast, Luke 7:30 records: "But the Pharisees and the lawyers rejected the purpose of God, for themselves, not having been baptized by him." As a sinful being, a person who does not get baptized is therefore *rejecting* what God has planned for him or her. Infants are no exception. To not baptize infants is *like the Pharisees, rejecting* what God has planned for our littlest ones. Infants are baptized so that God's will for all may be done for them as well.

Acts and the Epistles

The promise of salvation through baptism is for *all*. When the church was born, infants were included in baptism as well. Acts 2:38 says: "Repent, and be baptized every one of you in the name of Jesus Christ for the forgiveness of your sins; and you shall receive the gift of the Holy Spirit." And what does the very next verse, Acts 2:39, say? "For the promise is to *you and to your children* and to all that are far off, every one whom the Lord our God calls to him." The word for children used here is "*teknois*" which includes children of any age, even infants. But does that mean the people's own children? If the promise is for their children, it would include their babies.

But could the promise here refer to their more distant descendants? In other words, could the promise refer to their descendants in general? In that case, age would not be the issue. But if that route is taken, the promise of the Spirit and forgiveness would be given *apart* from the person's own repentance. A distant descendant would be given the Spirit and forgiveness on the basis of a *distant ancestor's* faith! And who would propose that *all* of these people's descendants through history would automatically be given these blessings? That wouldn't make any sense at all of this passage!

Rather, Peter is relaying this promise to *those present* who had heard his gospel message and anyone else who will "repent and be baptized." *These and their children* are given the promise. Jeremias writes of verse 39:

> The phrase "you and your children" with its variants . . . is a formula on the same lines as "you and your houses," which has already been discussed; it is a biblical expression like the latter and often alternates with it. Both phrases express completeness and both admit of no restriction. In its context "you and your children" (2:29) reproduces the list in 2:17 (Joel 2:28 [Hebrews 3:1]), "your sons and your daughters, your young men and your old men," which is likewise a paraphrase for the family in its completeness.[2]

The promise of the Holy Spirit was also for the children and infants present. They were to be baptized with their parents. That way they would receive the Holy Spirit and the forgiveness of sins. They too would become members of God's newly-born church!

So when Paul wrote to the Ephesian church (6:1-3), he wrote directly also to the "children" (*teknois*). Again, the word "*teknois*" includes also infants. So infants are members of God's church. And yet only a few verses before in Ephesians 5:25,26, Paul says: "Christ loved the church and gave himself for it to make it holy by washing it clean with water by the Word." Christ's baptism is for the church. Infants, then, should be baptized and so cleansed by the "washing of water by the Word." In the same way, children are identified as members of the Colossian church (Colossians 3:20). And there too, membership in the church is given through baptism (Colossians 2:12,19).

In Acts 26:22 Paul is brought before King Agrippa for a hearing. Paul describes his conversion on the Damascus road and his work to bring the gospel to the "small and great." Both "small" and "great" in the Greek refer to age. That Acts 26:22 is a reference to children and infants is shown also by the phrase "*mikroi kai megaloi*" (small and great) itself. Wherever this phrase is used in Scripture, it refers to *each and every one*. No one is excluded, whether infant or adult. For example, in Acts 8:10: "And they gave heed to him, *from the least to the greatest* . . . ." Hebrews 8:11: "They will all know me from the least to the greatest." Revelation 13:16: "Also it causes *all, both small and great,* both rich and poor, both free and slave . . . ." Revelation 19:5: "Praise our God, all you his servants, you who fear him, *small and great*." The usage of "small and great" emphasizes *all-inclusiveness*. Where the phrase is used, *all people* (infants also) must be seen as in the realm and meaning of the passage.

John says in 1 John 2:12,13: "I am writing to you, little children (*teknia*), because your sins are forgiven for his sake . . . . I write you, children (*paidia*), because you know the Father." John calls the people in the church "little children" (*teknia*). But then he addresses the little children *per se* using the word "*paidia*." "*Paidia*" was the same word used to describe the very small children brought to the arms of Jesus. Since John is writing to members of the church, he must consider children and infants as members too. Yet a man becomes a member of God's Kingdom in John's Gospel by being baptized (John 3:5,6). So again, infants and small children must have been baptized members of the church and not excluded as the opponents of infant baptism would have us believe. It is wrong, then, to deny infants their baptism when they are included in the other aspects of the church.

In Revelation 13:6-16 John mentions those who do not have their names in the book of life and uses the words "both small and great." These are the same words Paul used before Agrippa. The words "small" and "great" do not commonly mean size in the Greek but age. And the phrase itself is *all-inclusive*. Revelation 19:5 refers to those who fear him, both "great and small": "And from the throne came a voice crying, 'Praise our God, all you his servants, you who fear him, small and great.' " Infants are among those saved in heaven as well as those lost in hell. Revelation 20:12,15 tells of the "small and great" before the throne of God:

> And I saw the dead, *great and small*, standing before the throne, and the books were opened. Also another book was opened which is the book of life. And the dead were judged by what was written in the books, by what they had done. . . . and if any one's name was not found written in the book of life, he was thrown into the lake of fire.

So if the youngest are to be judged before God with some lost and others saved, then God's kingdom is on the line for even the littlest. And John has already explained how to enter the kingdom: ". . . unless one is born of water and the Spirit, he cannot enter the kingdom of God." This is God's means that he has entrusted to men whereby infants, too, may become members of God's family of faith.

David Scaer points out the connection between making disciples and baptizing and teaching:

> Making disciples out of all nations according to the command of Jesus in the last chapter of Matthew includes baptizing and teaching. There St. Paul says that he is using this two-pronged approach wherever he is sent. And the objects of this activity are children, yes, even the very youngest of them. St. Paul told King Agrippa that part of his activity was the baptizing of children. They too were capable of the message of salvation which St. Paul says includes the suffering of Christ, his resurrection from the dead, and the proclamation of this message to both the people of God and the Gentiles.[3]

Baptism, then, is the first step in an ongoing process of growth in the family of God, that family which includes the very young as well as the aged.

Baptism, as Peter said in Acts 2:38, is full of God's promises for the youngest. In baptism, they receive the full forgiveness of their sins, sins of which they are unconscious. And they receive the gift of the Holy Spirit who preserves them in the Lord Jesus. And God is always faithful in his promises. For this, parents can only rejoice and praise the Lord, a Lord who cares for *all*, even the tiniest of people!

10.

THE TESTIMONY OF THE EARLY CHURCH

While the Scriptures bear infant baptism out, so also does the history of the church. Many people who oppose infant baptism do not realize that it has been the historic practice of the Christian church. From the very first century of the church, while the apostles were still alive, infants were being baptized. The church already saw baptism as the means by which infants entered into the new life in Christ and the family of God. A brief overview of this history is in order.

The first two centuries

What makes this history difficult at first is that the earliest Christian writers do not really address infant baptism *per se*. Some believe that this is because infant baptism was not being practiced. But one might also conclude that it was because the practice was very common. No one felt that it needed to be defended. So which option is correct? If infant baptism were not being practiced, when later writers first mention it, wouldn't they attack it as a new and false practice? Wouldn't they attest that the church has never baptized babies? And finally, what sort of indirect evidence for one or the other is there from the earlier writers? And what does that evidence indicate?

While the first mention of infant baptism comes later in the second century, the earlier Christian writers do give some indirect help. For example, consider Justin Martyr. Justin Martyr lived from about A.D. 89 to 166. He was a philosopher and had studied the various schools of philosophy of the day. Justin finally concluded that Christianity is the true philosophy. So he set about to defend his new faith. He describes his conversion in the *Dialog with Trypho the Jew*. There he also calls baptism the circumcision of the New Testament.[1]

Justin Martyr defended his new faith in his *First* and *Second Apology*. These were addressed to Antoninus Pius, the Roman emperor. In the *Second Apology* he wrote: "And many, both men and women, who have been Christ's disciples [lit. *made disciples*] *from childhood* [*ek paidon*], remain pure [virginal] at the age of sixty or seventy years."[2] He used the same verb, "*mathateuein*," which Christ used in the baptismal command of Matthew 28:19.[3] Flemington adds:

> Further, Justin's use of the verb in the aorist [simple past] tense suggests that the emphasis here is not upon a continuous period of instruction in the faith, but rather upon a particular moment at which these men and women in their childhood entered the status of "discipleship." Thus the most natural interpretation of the passage seems to involve the baptism of these people as infants.[4]

If so, this means that infant baptism was practiced during Justin Martyr's lifetime and before (A.D. 80—90), while the Apostle John was still living. From birth, then, these people had remained pure, having been made disciples by infant baptism.

Another great figure in this early second century period was Polycarp. Irenaeus, a later second century writer, reports that Polycarp was a student of John the Apostle.[5] Polycarp was martyred for his Christian beliefs. The church over which he was bishop, Smyrna in Asia Minor, described his death in *The Martyrdom of Polycarp*. They wrote the account shortly after his death in A.D. 167 or 168.[6] At the trial before his martyrdom, Polycarp testified that he had been serving the Lord for 86 years.[7] That would point to the year A.D. 82 as when he began his service. Eighty-six years must indicate Polycarp's infancy. Between A.D. 157 and 161 Polycarp made a trip to visit Bishop Anicetus at Rome. If Polycarp was 86 years old when he died, the trip would have been when he was in his late seventies. But if Polycarp lived to be over ninety years old (and thus had served the Lord since, say, age four), his trip would have been when he was in his eighties. Such a difficult journey would demand that Polycarp be younger. "Eighty six years" is thus a reference to his age. According to Joachim Jeremias, this fact and

> . . . the other dates of Polycarp's life known to us make it extremely likely that eighty-six, the number of years, indicates his age . . . . the words "service of Christ" for eighty-six years supports a baptism soon after his birth rather than one as a child "of maturer years". . . . [8]

Both Polycarp and Justin Martyr were born in the latter half of the first century. This traces infant baptism back to the time of the apostles themselves.

When infant baptism is first directly addressed in the early church's writings, the authors see baptism as the standard custom going back to the apostles. No one thought otherwise. With regard to the later second century, Flemington points out: "The first clear reference to infant baptism occurs in a passage of Irenaeus (*circa* A.D. 185)."[9] Irenaeus was born between 140 and 160 A.D. in Asia Minor and knew Polycarp. He later became the bishop of Lyon in Gaul. He defended the faith against the errors of his day, while also seeking unity and peace. He is said to have died a martyr. Irenaeus, in one of his writings, describes how Christ saves both young and old alike: "For he came to save all through himself; all, that is, who through him are born again unto God, infants, and little ones, and boys, and youths, and old men."[10] "Born again unto God" (*renascunter in Deum*) is a synonym for "is baptized" in Irenaeus' writings.[11] Thus, Irenaeus defended baptism as the rebirth, whereby infants are born again unto God.

Tertullian was a contemporary of Irenaeus. While Irenaeus served in Gaul, Tertullian lived in Carthage, North Africa. He was born in A.D. 150. Around A.D. 200 to 206 he wrote *De Baptismo*. In chapter 18 he opposes the baptism of the infants of new converts. Tertullian affirms Matthew 19:14 ("Forbid them not to come to me") as the basis for infant baptism. Except when in an emergency, infant baptism placed too much of a burden on the godparents. They might die or have bad tendencies. Tertullian did not believe in original sin. So he had no objection if in these cases the infant baptisms were delayed. He just wondered how wise it is to baptize the children of pagans joining the church. But in the case of the children of Christians, Tertullian argues *for* infant baptism. He writes in regard to 1 Corinthians 7:14 that these children are "holy."[12] And one cannot be holy, for Tertullian, unless born of water and the spirit. Baptism cleanses the infant's soul. Here Tertullian affirms infant baptism.[13] And he attested that the baptism of babies was the standard practice at that time and *not* an innovation.[14]

What makes Tertullian so critical is that those who oppose infant baptism place a high value on his testimony. Tertullian is the only one in the first three centuries of the church who expressed any problems with infant baptism (though only in certain cases). Flemington shows the problems with this sort of reading of Tertullian:

> Yet nowhere did Tertullian produce what would have been a conclusive argument against the practice, namely that infant baptism was not a usage of apostolic days, nor did he anywhere so much as suggest such a possibility.[15]

While Tertullian opposed it in certain cases, he never even hinted at the possibility of infant baptism being of later origin. This clearly shows that infant baptism was the historic practice of the Christian church from the apostolic age.

Other writers from this period would include Hippolytus (215-220) who in his *Apostolic Tradition* spoke of entire households being baptized. This included the children who cannot answer for themselves.[16] Jeremias explains: "We are told that it took place in three parts (children, men, women) and that the parents said the baptismal confession for the smallest children."[17] According to the best evidence, Aristides' *Apology* is dated in the second century. It too mentioned household baptisms. All the evidence indicates that infant baptism was the accepted practice from the time of the apostles.

The third century

In the third century, Cyprian was the bishop of Carthage until his death in A.D. 258. He knew and was influenced by Tertullian (who also lived in Carthage).

Cyprian rebuked a presbyter in Numidia who taught that children should not be baptized until after their eighth day (as was the case with circumcision):

> And therefore, dearest brother, this was our opinion in council, that by us no one ought to be hindered from baptism and from the grace of God, who is merciful and kind and loving to all. Which, since it is to be observed and maintained in respect of all, we think is to be observed in respect of infants, and newly-born persons . . . . [18]

Flemington comments:

> The whole tone of the letter makes it clear that infant baptism itself was an accepted practice of the church and one that needed no arguments to be produced in its support. In the absence of any church pronouncement expressly authorizing its practice, it is reasonable to suppose that its beginnings go back to very early times.[19]

Also in the third century was Origen (184-254), a prolific writer who also founded a theological school in Caesarea. Origen wrote of infant baptism:

> The church has received from the apostles the custom of administering baptism even to infants. For those who have been entrusted with the secrets of the divine mysteries knew well that all are tainted with the stain of original sin, which must be washed off by the water and the Spirit. (In *Rom. Com.* 5,9 EH 249)[20]

Origen continued, "Infants are to be baptized for the remission of sins." Three times in his writings Origen discussed infant baptism and claimed that the practice originated with the apostles.[21] Jeremias writes:

> Origen presupposes that the practice of infant
> baptism is so natural and undisputed that it can
> provide extra support to underpin his assertion
> based on Scripture that newborn children are
> tainted by sin.[22]

In his writings, Origen was unaware of any conflict
whether infants should be baptized or not. He even used
infant baptism as an assumed premise, not needing any
qualification or defense. From infant baptism, Origen
felt he could argue original sin. Again, the evidence from
the third century shows that infant baptism was a continued practice from apostolic times.

Archaeological evidence, when available, buttresses
the case for infant baptism in the early church. A third
century tombstone inscription in Latin reads:

> Dedicated to the departed. Florentius made this
> inscription for his worthy son Apronianus who
> lived one year and nine months and five days. As
> he was truly loved by his grandmother and she
> knew that his death was imminent, she asked the
> church that he might depart from the world as a
> believer.

Jeremias comments that "it reports an occurrence
which quite certainly was not unique":

> We have here a case of private baptism in an
> emergency, which was administered to the one-
> and-three-quarter-year-old Apronianus in time
> and enabled him to die as a believer (*fidelis*). The
> very fact that it was the grandmother who urged
> that her darling should be baptized before his
> death, makes it in the highest degree probable

that the father of the child, Florentius, was a pagan. This conjecture is confirmed by the formula in the first line, strikingly pagan for a Christian third-century catacomb inscription: *dis manibus sacrum* ["dms"—"dedicated to the departed"]. We have thus in the Apronianus inscription evidence before us for a missionary baptism administered to a twenty-one month old dying non-Christian infant.[23]

Another tombstone inscription from the third century read: "I, Zosimus, a believer from believers, lie here having lived 2 years, 1 month, 25 days." Jeremias elaborates on the significance of the inscription:

Zosimus . . . is described as *pistos ek piston* and thereby as the baptized child of Christian parents, since, according to the established usage, the word *pistos* describes a baptized person (as contrasted with a catechumen).[24]

Jeremias includes a lengthy discussion of other tombstone inscriptions that show infant baptism as the normal practice of the third century. But why wasn't there such evidence before A.D. 200? There simply were no Christian epitaphs earlier than A.D. 200. But when the Christian inscriptions begin, infant baptism is well attested.[25] Many of Jeremias' examples were cases of emergency infant baptism on the day of a child's death. In the fourth century it was often customary to include mention of the emergency baptism on the tombstone inscription. Jeremias concludes from the archaeological evidence:

Delay of baptism in the case of Christian children was wholly unknown in the primitive church. It is not until the year 329-30 [fourth century] that we

have certain evidence of a case of Christian parents letting their children grow up unbaptized.[26]

This was about the same time as the fourth century
controversy on infant baptism. Before then, however,
such controversy would have been unheard of.

The fourth century

In the fourth century the first serious conflict
emerged in the church challenging t!he custom of infant
baptism. Yet even the heretic Pelagius (born in A.D. 330),
while not accepting original sin, said in his writings that
he had never even heard of people asserting that infants
should not be baptized: "And then who is so impious as
to wish to exclude infants from the kingdom of heaven,
by forbidding them to be baptized and to be born again
in Christ?"[27] Augustine (354-430) wrote: "The Pelagians
have never dared deny infant baptism, because they
know that if they had denied it, they would have to fight
quite manifestly with the whole church." Augustine further attested that "the whole church is making use of it"
and that the custom of baptizing infants "stems from the
holy apostles."[28] In Augustine's *Tenth Sermon* he admonished his listeners: "Let no one mislead you by false doctrine. The baptism of children the church has practiced
at all times . . . and has guarded it to this day continu-
ously." The Council at Carthage (418) decreed: "Whoever
denies that newly born children are to be baptized, let
him be accursed." Jeremias adds with regard to the
fourth century:

> But the Church Orders are by no means our only
> evidence. For the West we have also the decisions
> of the Synod of Elvira in southern Spain, and
> above all tombstone inscriptions, proving that in
> the fourth century as before, infant baptism was

administered to the children of Christian parents, since we find at this period numerous inscriptions concerning infants who were obviously baptized at birth.[29]

In the Eastern church in the fourth century, where certain baptisms were postponed, newborn infants were still baptized "as the normal practice."[30] Even the fourth century heretics would have their babies baptized. And after the conflict subsided, the available historical evidence shows that infant children were again baptized as the accepted practice:

After about 365 the literary sources begin to flow freely. The baptism of newborn infants is cited as a well-established custom, enjoined and theologically justified, as if nothing had happened.[31]

Finally, the challenge to infant baptism was overcome by the Council of Carthage, with the help of Augustine. Sasse concludes:

What we know of the history of the church indicates much rather that in the early church both forms of baptism, the baptism of adults and infant baptism, always existed side by side, just as they do today in the mission fields. This can only mean that infant baptism must go back to the time of the apostles. It would have been included in the practice of baptizing whole families to which the New Testament gives witness, even though children are not explicitly mentioned.[32]

As a helpful additional point, Oscar Cullman writes:

. . . I should like, on the other hand, with all force to emphasize at the outset that there are in the

New Testament decidedly *fewer traces, indeed none at all, of the baptism of adults born of Christians and brought up by them.* Chronologically, such a case would have been possible about the year 50, if not earlier, that is, certainly within New Testament times.[33]

Cullman concludes:

Those who dispute the Biblical character of infant baptism have therefore to reckon with the fact that *adult baptism for sons and daughters born of Christian parents, which they recommend, is even worse attested by the New Testament than infant baptism . . . and indeed lacks any kind of proof.*[34]

No one in the first four centuries ever argued that infant baptism was not the established, historic practice from the apostles. That infant baptism was never even doctrinally questioned, excepting Tertullian and the fourth century critics, shows that the Fathers considered it the proper practice. Only with the Anabaptists in the later Reformation period was infant baptism seriously attacked. From then and up to the present, the doctrine has been in serious jeopardy. It is unfortunate that what was so clear to the early church fathers from Scripture has now been so distorted.

Meanwhile, the spiritual life of infants is at stake. May every Christian parent be as concerned about his or her child's eternal destiny as these early Christians! God's wonderful "means of grace" for infants was not only for those early Christian parents but for us today as well!

11.

A SUMMARY OF THE BIBLICAL MATERIAL

1. Christ commanded that *all nations* are to be baptized (Matthew 28:18-20). Note: "to baptize" derives imperative force from the main verb "to make disciples" and describes the means whereby disciples are made.
   A. Children are to be baptized if they are to be made disciples.
   B. The ordinance to teach is fulfilled by a Christian upbringing.
   C. No exceptions are made to the emphatic command ("all").
   D. "Nations" is better translated "people." No particular people is to be excluded from the command to baptize, including infants. *Nowhere in Scripture is infant baptism rejected.* The absence of such, in light of the strong command, necessitates baptism.
   E. Children are considered members of "nations" and "peoples" in the Old Testament—Exodus 11:5; Joshua 8:35; 1 Samuel 15:3; 2 Chronicles 20:13; Nehemiah 12:43; Isaiah 13:16; 14:21; 20:4; Jeremiah 18:21; 38:23; Lamentations 2:11,19; Ezekiel 9:6;

Hosea 2:4; Joel 2:16; Nahum 3:10. See also Exodus 20:5.

F. The context of children and little ones as members of the kingdom, particularly in Matthew 18 and 19 shows that Matthew 28:18-20 is for the little ones.

2. Paul compared and made an analogy between baptism and circumcision. Since circumcision is for infants, so also is baptism—Colossians 2:11-13.

A. Paul *explicitly* calls baptism the circumcision of Christ.

B. Infants were circumcised—Genesis 17:9-14; Leviticus 12:3—thus, infants are to be baptized. Would not any analogy made between circumcision and baptism immediately call to mind an understanding of infant baptism since infants were the usual recipients of circumcision in Israel?

C. This conclusion is strengthened by the many similarities between baptism and circumcision.

D. Circumcision was established and given on the basis of Abraham's *faith* (Romans 4:11); so baptism is based in adults on faith.

E. Circumcision is not valid without faith; so it is with baptism also. (Deuteronomy 30:6; Jeremiah 4:4; 9:26).

F. Yet infants were circumcised; so infants should be baptized.

G. Men were circumcised in the Old Testament as circumcision pointed to the male Messiah who would come from Israel; baptism is based on Christ's completed work opening salvation to *all*.

3. Old Testament washings were never restricted to adults but were for anyone, including children. They were for the *whole Israelite nation*—Exodus 29:4; Leviticus 14:7-9; 16:14-19; Numbers 19:7,13-21; Ezekiel 36:25.

4. Paul says that *all* of Israel was baptized in the Red Sea—1 Corinthians 10:1,2.
   A. Note the repeated emphatic "all" in the passage.
   B. Children and infants were included; therefore infants are baptized.

5. Jewish proselyte baptism before Christ included infants.
   A. Jewish rabbinic tradition, based on an oral tradition from before the time of Christ, teaches proselyte baptism. This is in accordance with direct evidence also from before Christ.
   B. Children were always to be baptized with their parents in Jewish proselyte baptism.
   C. Biblical evidence corresponds with this. Matthew 23:15 teaches that the Pharisees were already vigorous in their desires to win proselytes. John 1:24 speaks of John the Baptist's baptism, a true proselyte baptism. The Pharisees do not question John's practice of proselyte baptism, thus giving evidence that they were already familiar with the practice.

6. *Entire* families were baptized in the book of Acts.
   A. The word used for "household" in the New Testament always includes the children and infants—see the Greek Old Testament (Septuagint)—Genesis 17:23; 45:18,19; 46:6,7; 1 Samuel 22:16-19.
   B. The Jews considered the entire family a corporate unit—Genesis 7:1; 17:23; 34:30; 36:6; Exodus 1:1; Numbers 18:31; Deuteronomy 12:7; 14:2; 15:20; Joshua 24:15; Judges 18:25; 1 Samuel 1:21; 27:3; 2 Samuel 2:3; 15:16; Esther 4:14.
   C. Note that in each of the Acts accounts—Acts 10:24,48; 11:14; 16:15; 16:28-36; 18:8—the word "household" occurs repeatedly, which coupled with

the Jewish understanding of a household requires infant baptism.

D. The additional use of "all" accompanying the Acts texts further strengthens the mandatory nature of infant baptism. The texts use strict, emphatic language in describing the entire households' baptisms. No exceptions are made. Though infants are not specifically singled out among the baptized, neither are the other adults. We should not expect infants to be singled out since only the head of the households and their significance and belief are mentioned. The texts have already been explicit in their descriptions that *all* were baptized. Even if children were not present in the Acts households, that "households" were baptized without qualification and with vigorous emphasis demands infant baptism in households today.

7. Children are born in sin (original sin) which requires the cleansing water of baptism.
   A. Original sin—Genesis 1:20; 5:3; 8:21; Job 14:1-4; 15:14; 25:4; Psalm 25:7; 51; 58:3; Proverbs 20:9-11; Ecclesiastes 7:20; Matthew 7:17; Romans 3:10-12; 5; 7:14-25; 8:7,8; Ephesians 2:1-3; 1 Corinthians 2:14.
   B. John 3:5-8 explains that original sin can only be confronted in the water of baptism. The single "and" and the single "of" in the Greek text demonstrates that one is born "of water and Spirit" and *not* "of water and of the Spirit" as if there were two separate births as some have suggested. See also the context of water baptism in John 3:22,23 immediately following this discussion. Infants must be born "of water and the Spirit" if they are to be saved from their birth in the flesh (sin).

8. Baptism saves and so infants should be baptized for their salvation—Mark 16:16; John 3:6; Acts 2:38f; 22:16; Romans 6:3-14; 1 Corinthians 6:11; Ephesians 5:25-27; Colossians 2:12; Titus 3:5-7; 1 Peter 3:20,21. If 1 Corinthians 7:14 proves that infants do not need to be baptized since a parent believes, then neither does the unbelieving spouse need baptism—is he or she saved, too?

9. Infants can believe. (Faith is a necessary accompaniment.)
   A. Salvation is entirely the work of God—Jeremiah 6:10; Ezekiel 12:2; Zechariah 7:11; Matthew 13:15; 19:25; John 15:16; Romans 7:14-20; 8:7; 9; 1 Corinthians 2; Ephesians 1; 2:8,9; 2 Timothy 4:4. The Spirit supernaturally opens our hearts to faith. Faith is *received* and not accepted. So God can create faith in the infant even as he does with the adult.
   B. Children and infants are capable of receiving the gift of faith because they are examples for adults of how to enter into God's kingdom (of grace)— Matthew 18; 19; Luke 18:15-17. Luke identifies these children as "infants." And Christ specifically says that little children, including babies according to Luke, *believe* in the phrase "these little ones which believe in me." These little ones are adults' *examples* as to how to enter into God's kingdom, thus showing that they are already prime recipients of salvation.
   C. See also Psalms 22:9,10; 71:5,6; Matthew 21:15,16; Luke 1:15,41,44; 10:21; Romans 8:1-6; 1 Corinthians 12:3; 1 Peter 2:2. Such passages *explicitly* attribute faith to infants.
   D. Faith in Christ and baptism is the *only* way to be saved according to the Scriptures. If infants cannot

113

believe and so have faith, how else can they be saved from the effects of sin? Are those who deny infant faith saying that no infants can be saved since they are not old enough to have true faith? Is not this the logical implication of the denial of infant faith in view of the scriptural fact that it is only by faith in Christ that one is saved (Acts 4:12; Ephesians 2:8,9)?

E. A final issue to be resolved concerns which babies to baptize, that is, which have faith. Since *Christ used infants and small children as examples of how adults must become to enter God's kingdom,* it must be concluded that infants and small children *receive the gift of God's grace freely whenever it is offered to them.* So *when the child is baptized,* adults need only rest on the promise of the cleansing from sin that comes through baptism confident that *infants will receive such cleansing freely.* For it is to "such as these" that the kingdom of heaven belongs. In baptism the Spirit works faith in the unconscious infant or small child. In the conscious adult, repentance and confession are necessary first before baptism that their faith may be attested to. In the child this faith is created through baptism, since infants and small children are examples of how to receive faith and the kingdom.

Note: While faith and conscious reasoning must be distinguished from each other, it is the requirement of Scripture that children be brought up in the faith. In this, the unconscious infant baptismal faith is transformed into a conscious faith. For this reason, as a rule, only the children of Christian parents are baptized, so that these little ones who have received him in the cleansing water of baptism may not fall away from their baptismal grace as they grow into the age of conscious discretion. A baptized child must be brought up "in the nurture and admonition of the Lord" and is to be reminded of the blessings he or she received in baptism (see 3). The infants of Christian parents are all to be baptized since it is such as the little children and infants who receive the kingdom of heaven and the gift of faith. Baptism is the means of grace whereby infants' sins are washed away. Infants are to be baptized to apply the words of Matthew 19:13-15 (Mark 10:13-16; Luke 18:15-17) to let the children come to him. Galatians 3:27 promises that *in baptism* Christ is put on. To bring infants to Christ, then, requires baptism.

10. Further arguments:
   A. The Acts 2:39 baptismal promise is for the *children.*
   B. Paul addresses the "children" in Ephesus (with a word that includes infants)—Ephesians 6:1-3. So the Ephesians 5:25,26 baptismal washing is also for children and infants in the church. Similarly, Colossians 3:20 addresses children in the congregation, yet congregation membership comes through baptism (Colossians 2:12,19).

11. Paul and John:
   A. Acts 26:22—"Small and great" are ministered to, which includes *all* people whenever used no matter what sort (Acts 8:10; Revelation 19:5; 20:12,15, etc.).
   B. John specifically addresses the children (with a word inclusive of infants) in 1 John 2:12,13. Revelation 13:6-16 speaks of the children (and infants) whose names are not in the book of life by means, again, of the phrase "small and great" (see also Revelation 19:5; 20:12,15).
   C. Paul and Christ were both baptized (Acts 9:18; Matthew 3:16) further showing that baptism is for all.

D. Matthew 3:5,6 records *all Judea and the whole Jordan valley* being baptized. Given the use of "all" and the Jewish understanding of infant proselyte baptism, why wasn't the exclusion of infants explicitly mentioned if such were the case?

12. Infant baptism was never seriously attacked until the fourth century. No early Christian writer questioned that infant baptism was the accepted practice from the apostolic age. Grave markers from the third century (when they are first found in Christian history) immediately attested to infant baptism. Infant baptism is the historic practice of the Christian church from apostolic times.

Infant baptism is never spoken against in Scripture, while the baptism of all is strongly commanded. While infants were not singled out in Christ's baptismal command, neither was any other particular group.

The pointlessness of arguing that there is no explicit command to baptize infants may be shown by an analogy. There is no command to commune women. So should only men commune (since there were no women at the Last Supper)? Nonsense! Rather, the Scriptures have a whole theology and understanding of communion as given to the church. So, we have seen, the Scriptures have a very extensive and developed understanding of how infants and children fit into God's divine plan. And we can see that salvation and God's "means of grace" are for *ALL*, even the smallest.

They, too, are to be part of the family of God through baptism!

CONCLUSION:
THE RICHES OF GOD'S GRACE

Scripture presents a great deal of information about God's plan for the littlest. The Scriptures also have much to say about baptism in God's plan. So we have seen from various biblical lines of reasoning how God would also have our infants and smallest children baptized. Surely, if we are to deny the truth of infant baptism, we must be able to give a good answer to the evidence of Scripture here presented. Otherwise, by not allowing infants to be cleansed of their sins in baptism, would we not fall under the jurisdiction of those words Jesus spoke to *his disciples* in Mark 9:42: "If anyone leads into sin one of these little ones which believe in me, it would be better for him to have a big millstone hung around his neck and be thrown into the lake"?

When one considers the riches of God's grace that are offered in baptism, knowing that infants receive such grace freely, it is inconceivable that a Christian parent or pastor would withhold baptism from an infant. Infants receive the full blessings of baptism and the parents and the church gain the assurance of their baby's eternal well-being. God entrusted baptism to his church that *all* people might be made his disciples and so experience the marvelous riches of his grace and salvation. Infant baptism is as much a part of the Church's mission as the very gospel of Christ. For in infant baptism the Holy Spirit creates a saving faith in Jesus Christ. And that's precious!

LINGERING QUESTIONS

In the 17 years since Northwestern Publishing House graciously published the first edition of this book, many have asked about the young woman in the introduction. No, I never convinced her of infant baptism. The Lord had different plans.

I met the love of my life seven years later at the institution that granted my Ph.D. She was the director of financial aid—obviously a very important person for someone with financial need! So I applied for the Spousal Scholarship, literally. The paperwork was fierce, but the reward was beyond my greatest dreams. Susan and I now have three wonderful children: Peter, Paul, and Sara. The Lord saw fit that I was able to serve as the instrument for his baptizing of Paul and Sara. I treasure the memories of those moments!

As I was talking with my college friend about baptism all those years ago, the Lord was preparing me for my future wife. Susan came from a Christian tradition that was different from my own, and when I met her, I had more experience with friendly disagreements. She still often reminds me that "people convinced against their will are of the same opinion still." The Lord must prepare a person's heart to hear his Word. Sometimes the soil may not be ready for the seed to bear fruit. It is not for us to question the harvest. We only have to cast the seed and pray that it will be fruitful. We have God's promise that it will be fruitful, even if we don't always see the visible results (Isaiah 55:11). At the same time, it certainly helps to remove as many obstacles as possible to the hearing of his Word.

Since the first edition of *Baptized Into God's Family*, readers have asked me about several matters that they wish I had said more about. This second edition allows me to answer a few of those lingering questions. For instance, some have wondered about whether the real power is not in the waters of baptism but rather in a second experience referred to as the "baptism of the Holy Spirit" (see section 1 below). They point out that the Apostle Paul seems to minimize the importance of baptism in 1 Corinthians 1:14-17 (see section 2). Some think that since baptism is only valid with repentance—a conscious act on the part of the individual—infants should not be baptized since they are incapable of this decision (see section 3). Baptized infants who, once grown, publicly leave the faith pose a problem for those who think that once an individual is saved, that person cannot fall away from faith. They conclude that infants must not be saved by baptism (see section 4). Finally, still others wonder if they should be baptized again since their infant baptisms were not by means of immersion (see section 5). May what follows, by the Lord's gracious power, help people further treasure the waters of baptism for even the littlest ones among us!

1. The baptism of the Holy Spirit

Infant baptism was not the only issue that divided my college friend and me. I was a Lutheran and she a Pentecostal. She urged me to experience the moment of *real* power for a Christian—not water baptism. She told me all about the "baptism of the Holy Spirit." This was a strange, new doctrine for me. I had not heard of it before. She took me through the book of Acts and talked about how believers received a full empowering of the Holy Spirit. Speaking in tongues was God's sign that a person had received this great blessing. In Acts 10, Cornelius and his household were already believers in Jesus Christ when they received a special outpouring of the Holy Spirit. The Samaritans in Acts 8 believed and were baptized but did not receive the Holy Spirit until later. The Ephesian "disciples" in Acts 19:1-7 had not even heard of the Holy Spirit. Each of these groups of believers still needed to receive the power of the Holy Spirit. Their "second experiences" came well after their conversions.

Does Acts really teach a "second experience" of the Spirit after a person becomes a believer and is baptized? Actually, a closer look at Acts shows that Luke ties the Spirit's power and presence not to some second experience but to *water baptism!* In Acts 2:38, Peter urged the people, "Repent and be baptized, every one of you, in the name of Jesus Christ for the forgiveness of your sins." Notice that the sentence goes on! "And you will receive the gift of the Holy Spirit." The gift of the Holy Spirit is simply a promise to every baptized believer. Christians don't have to pray for or strive for the Holy Spirit. His power is already theirs! What follows in the book of Acts reinforces this point. The Spirit accompanies belief and, yes, water baptism. In Acts 10:44, when the Holy Spirit fell upon Cornelius' household, what were the first words from Peter's lips? "Can anyone keep these people from being *baptized* with *water?* They have received the Holy Spirit just as we have" (verse 47). And so Peter "ordered" them to be baptized with water. For Peter, water baptism and the Holy Spirit went hand in hand. Whether the baptism preceded the Holy Spirit or the Holy Spirit preceded the baptism, there could not be one without the other (cf. John 3:8). In Acts 19 the Apostle Paul came across some "disciples" on the road to Ephesus. He asked them, "Did you receive the Holy Spirit when you believed?" (verse 2). They answered that they had not even heard of the Holy Spirit. What was Paul's immediate diagnostic question? "Then what baptism did you receive?" (verse 3). For people who are lacking the Spirit's presence or power, Paul would have us ask them whether they were baptized in the name of the Triune God of power. The Holy Spirit comes in the context of water baptism.

The "disciples" in Acts 19 responded to Paul's diagnostic question that they had been baptized into John's baptism. John, however, had preached about the coming Christ who would baptize with the Holy Spirit (Luke 3:16). These people were entirely unaware of the Spirit whom John had mentioned. So Paul reviewed John's teaching about the more powerful one who was coming. Luke's Gospel conveys the distinct impression that had these disciples received John's baptism properly, they should have already known about Jesus and the Spirit. Apollos in Acts 18:24-28 had been baptized by John and had taught with great power (literally "by the S/spirit") about Jesus Christ. Unlike Apollos, who did not need to be baptized again, this Ephesian group *did* need to be baptized. They had not actually received the baptism of John, since he had been baptizing with a view to the coming Savior. Their initial description as "disciples" is somewhat ironic (cf. Apollos). After being baptized in water, they shortly received the Spirit.

Acts 8 is the only instance for Luke where water baptism was not accompanied by the coming of the Spirit. The Samaritans believed and were baptized but were without the Holy Spirit. Luke, however, is careful to tip the reader off that the Samaritans *should have* received the Spirit with water baptism. The translations do not always convey the original Greek. To translate more literally, *"Not yet* had they received the Holy Spirit; their baptism was alone [unaccompanied]" (verse 16). In other words, the Samaritans had "not yet" received what they should have received. Their baptisms were unaccompanied. And yet that was not how it was supposed to be!

Why is it that in this instance the Spirit saw fit to delay his coming from the waters of baptism and Christian belief? The key is to examine Acts 8 in the entire context of Luke's writings. Acts 8 centers on the events in Samaria. The Evangelist Luke belabors more than any other Gospel writer the relationship between the Jews and their Samaritan neighbors. The Jews and the Samaritans had a history of bad blood going back several centuries. Matters weren't helped when some Samaritans snuck into the temple one night before Passover during the time of Jesus' childhood to spread bones. Luke tells the story of the good Samaritan (Luke 10:25-37). Luke also tells the story of the one leper who returned to give Jesus thanks after being cured—a Samaritan (Luke 17:11-19). Luke relays a sense of the prejudice and hatred that the Jews—even Jesus' own disciples—felt toward the Samaritans. In Luke 9:54, the disciple John and his brother wanted to call down fire on the Samaritans. The Lord rebuked the two brothers. But this was not Jesus' last word on the matter. Years later the Lord eventually *did* let John call down fire on the Samaritans. It wasn't the kind of fire John had expected. It was the fire of the *Holy Spirit* (Acts 8:15-17; cf. Luke 3:16; Acts 2:1-4). The Holy Spirit, by his delay, was forcing people torn apart for centuries by ethnic strife and hatred to be reconciled. The Spirit was creating a church in Jerusalem, Judea, *and Samaria,* even to the ends of the earth (Acts 1:8). This was to be a church that crossed *every* boundary. Nothing could stand in the Spirit's way—not even human prejudice![1] The delay of the Spirit after the Samaritans' baptisms was, therefore, a unique event at a pivotal moment in the history of God's people.

My college friend had urged me to experience "something more" in my spiritual life. She had wanted me to seek a "second experience" of the Spirit to enjoy his full power and strength. But the full power of the Holy Spirit was made available to me in my baptism, just as the book of Acts teaches. No baptized believer in Jesus Christ is in any way a lesser Christian or without power. No baptized Christian need look for "something more." No baptized Christian is a spiritual "have not." Christians do, however, need to recognize and claim each day the power that was given to them in the waters of baptism. By virtue of baptism, the Holy Spirit becomes a source of real spiritual strength in our Christian lives.

2. First Corinthians 1:14-17

If baptism is so powerful, many have wondered about 1 Corinthians 1:14-17. At first glance of these verses, it seems the Apostle Paul did not have a very high view of baptism. In the context, Paul was clearly upset with the Corinthians. They were divided into rival factions. Some were saying, "'I follow Paul'; another, 'I follow Apollos'; another, 'I follow Cephas'; still another, 'I follow Christ'" (verse 12). Paul asked in response, "Is Christ divided? Was Paul crucified for you? Were you baptized into the name of Paul?" (verse 13). This mention of baptism then prompted Paul to digress in verses 14-17:

> I am thankful that I did not baptize any of you except Crispus and Gaius, so no one can say that you were baptized into my name. (Yes, I also baptized the household of Stephanas; beyond that, I don't remember if I baptized anyone else.) For Christ did not send me to baptize, but to preach the gospel—not with words of human wisdom, lest the cross of Christ be emptied of its power.

Many have concluded from these four verses that Paul did not see baptism as an instrument of salvation. Here he seemed to distinguish baptism from what *really* saves, the proclamation of the gospel.

These verses only briefly raise the matter of baptism. Baptism was not Paul's main point in this context. The Corinthian church had become a personality cult. "Were you baptized into the name of Paul?" People were valuing their baptisms on the basis of the persons who had administered them. The ancient writer Plutarch quipped that status seekers are like ivy twining around a strong tree (*Moralia* 805 E.-F.). The early Christian writer Chrysostom commented that baptism "is not the work of the person baptizing, but of Him who is invoked in the baptism" (*Homily on the Epistle of Paul to the Corinthians* 3.6 [NPNF[1] 12:12]). The late second-century Christian writer Tertullian in his writing *On Baptism* (14) noted that Paul did indeed baptize people. In 1 Corinthians 1 the apostle was just glad that he had not baptized even more people lest he would have become the center of their personality cult. On the other hand, the people Paul baptized appear to have been of great consequence. Crispus may well have been the synagogue ruler mentioned in Acts 18:8. Gaius was probably the same man mentioned in Romans 16:23. They seem to have been very early converts and of some stature. In an ironic twist, if the Corinthians wanted to boast of who performed their baptisms, Paul could boast of whom he baptized.

What about Paul's apparent distinction between baptizing and proclaiming the gospel? Paul clearly stated in Romans 6:3-11 that baptism proclaims the gospel of Christ's death and resurrection. In 1 Corinthians 11:24-27, he said that the Lord's Supper proclaims Christ's death and resurrection. Paul was placing his emphasis in 1 Corinthians 1:16,17 on *performing* baptisms and *preaching eloquently* as actions that draw attention to the minister and his status. Instead of serving as instruments of the gospel's proclamation, baptisms and wise orations were, ironically, drawing the Corinthians' attention to the people involved. Paul preferred, for his part, the term "gospelize," translated rather literally. "Gospelize" does not draw attention to *how* the message is conveyed. "Gospelize" says nothing about the proclaimer. Paul did not come to employ wise, impressive words or to perform baptisms but rather to gospelize. First Corinthians 1:16,17 was to be focused entirely on the personality cults at Corinth. Paul was not making any claims about baptism as such, nor was he downplaying eloquent preaching as such. The danger is when, in practice, people wrongly sever baptism and preaching from Christ's cross. Human wisdom and boasting are vain and worthless substitutes. Since people had become the focus at Corinth, Paul was saying that he was glad that he had not baptized more. Administering water and delivering fancy orations have no power of their own apart from the cross of Christ. What a scandal when Christians gather together because of the preacher and not the message![2]

One must not go beyond what 1 Corinthians 1:16,17 actually says, nor should these verses be set against what Paul has taught elsewhere. Baptism is no mere symbolic rite, as many modern Christians are apt to think. In Romans 6:3-5, Paul treated baptism as the *means* by which the individual is united to Christ's saving death. The realism Paul assumed is typical for an ancient author. In an era of rationalism that is ever seeping into Christian circles, a modern person has difficulty envisioning a rite actually effecting something. Most ancients, for their part, did not doubt the presence of supernatural realities. Participants in pagan mystery rites believed that they were actually being united to the god or goddess. Paul warned of demonic realities in pagan meals (1 Corinthians 10:18-22). The Lord's Supper bore actual, tangible effects in people's bodies (1 Corinthians 11:29-32). The early Christians would have had no problem understanding baptism as actually uniting the baptized with Christ, as Paul himself claimed. Paul reminded the Corinthians in 1 Corinthians 15:29 that Christians receive baptism "with a view to" the resurrection from the dead. Baptism connects us to Christ's saving work and the promise of the resurrection![3]

3. Mark 16:16 and the necessity of repentance

Occasionally, a perceptive reader will ask me about Mark 16:16, which I drew upon in the first edition of this book as evidence of baptism's necessity: "Whoever believes and is baptized will be saved, but whoever does not believe will be condemned." They inquire that many of the earliest and most reliable manuscripts omit that verse and all that follows in chapter 16 after verse 8. A good point. Nevertheless, there is a possibility that the text of verse 16 may have been in the original copy of Mark. And Mark 16:16 is still an important witness to how the very first Christians understood baptism, even to how the Lord himself treated it. Mark 16:16 teaches that baptism is necessary for salvation, even if it is the lack of belief that damns. Mark 16:16 also summarizes in a nice way what can be shown about baptism on the basis of several other passages in Scripture.

Mark 16:16 does mention belief alongside baptism. In the early chapters of *Baptized Into God's Family,* I responded that belief is ascribed even to the youngest in the Bible and is God's miracle. Many readers over the years have wished I had said more about repentance. Isn't it true that a person must *repent* and be baptized? Isn't the conscious act of repentance the main thing? How can a baby repent? But as God saves, he meets each

127

of us where we are. God therefore moves the adult to repent, which includes a conscious turnabout. This action of an adult's repentance is no less a miracle of God than what God works in a baby. We should not place the emphasis on what *we* do. We must always place the emphasis on what *God* does. What we say about baptism, we must say about repentance. It is utterly miraculous. Just as faith is a miracle of God's creation through his Word (Romans 10:16,17; John 1:12,13), so also is the act of repentance. In Acts 5:31 God exalted Christ so that "he might *give* repentance and forgiveness of sins" (author's emphasis). In Acts 11:18, at word of the conversion of Cornelius' household, the Jerusalem believers "praised God, saying, 'So then, God has granted even the Gentiles repentance unto life.'" Repentance is a *gift of God!* It is God's supernatural creation.

Luke's Gospel makes the same point about repentance. The sinner who repents in Luke 15:3-7 is like a helpless sheep that falls on its knees in panic. The shepherd must find that lost sheep and carry the paralyzed animal on his shoulders back to the flock. In Luke 15:8-10 the sinner who repents is like an inanimate coin that can do absolutely nothing for itself. In the parable of the prodigal son, the younger son does not repent. No, while sitting in the pig sty, he is still calculating how to earn his way back into his father's good graces as a hired hand. Although "repent" is one of Luke's favorite terms, which he uses in the parallel parables in Luke 15:7 and 10, he does not use the term in the case of the prodigal son. This is no accident. Repentance is not a part of the younger son's desperate scheme to survive. Repentance is a father who embraces his lost son with his love. Repentance is a miracle wrought by God's overwhelming and powerful love. It should be no surprise, then, that Luke tells of *infants* being brought to Jesus as those to whom the kingdom of heaven belongs (Luke

18:15-17). Just as miraculous as the "little ones who believe in me" (Matthew 18:2,6), so is their divinely wrought repentance.

4. Once saved, always saved

My father-in-law struggles with infant baptism. Although his children and grandchildren were all baptized as infants, he does not believe baptism is anything more than a symbol of the children's entry into the church community. Baptism does not actually *do* anything for the infant. It does not save. As a former Lutheran, he has witnessed far too many people baptized as infants abandon their Christian confession. As he reads Scripture, it is clear to him that once a person genuinely becomes a believer in Christ, that person cannot fall away from faith. He reasons that baptism must not have saved those infants since if it had, they would not have fallen away from genuine salvation. In the first edition, I merely quoted four passages: Matthew 13:5-7,18,20-22; Hebrews 6:4-6; 10:26,27; 2 Peter 2:20-22. My father-in-law found the brief treatment less than convincing. A few further comments may prove helpful for those who are still struggling with this point.

In Matthew 13:20-22, Jesus explains the meaning of the seed that fell on the rocky ground in the parable of the sower: "The one who received the seed that fell on rocky places is the man who hears the word and at once receives it with joy. But since he has no root, he lasts only a short time. When trouble or persecution comes because of the word, he quickly falls away" (verses 20,21). As Jesus says in Luke's Gospel, "Those on the rock are the ones who receive the word with joy when they hear it, but they have no root. They believe for a while, but in the time of testing they fall away" (8:13). Jesus' words recorded in Luke make it clear that this seed actually believed.

"Believe" is a strong word in Luke's Gospel and the book of Acts. "Believe" never refers to false or less-than-genuine faith. A quick word study of a few instances will help. God rebuked Zechariah because he did not "believe" God's Word given to him through the angel Gabriel (Luke 1:20). In Luke 8:50, Jesus urged Jairus to "believe." His belief would mediate God's blessing and healing of his daughter. Jesus chided the disciples in Luke 24:25 for being "slow of heart to believe" what the prophets had said. Acts 2:44 uses the word "believers" to describe the first Christians after Pentecost. Likewise, Acts 4:4,32 and 5:14 all speak of those who "believed" the message of Christ and so were counted among the first Christians. Several passages refer to those who come to "believe" the gospel message or to the "believers" (Acts 9:42; 14:1,23; 15:5; 16:31; 17:12,34; 18:8,27). Acts 10:43 says that anyone "who believes in him receives forgiveness of sins through his name." Those who "believe" receive God's forgiveness. In Acts 11:21, a great many people "believed and turned to the Lord." In Acts 13:12, the proconsul believed, which was yet another victory for the Lord in Acts. In verse 39, it says, "Everyone who believes is justified from everything you could not be justified from by the law of Moses." In verse 41, the text speaks of scoffers who "never believe." Scoffers are defined by their *lack* of belief. In verse 48, "all who were appointed for eternal life believed." Belief here is the result of God's divine action from eternity. In Acts 19:2, Paul asked the Ephesian disciples if they received the Holy Spirit when they "believed." When he learned that they had not heard of the Holy Spirit, he immediately asked about their water baptism. He did not question their belief. In verse 4, Paul recognized that John had urged people to "believe" in Jesus. Acts 19:18, 21:20,25 all spoke positively of those who "believed." In Acts 22:19, Paul described his mission as a former antagonist who beat those who "believed" in the Lord. Unless the context specifies otherwise, the word "believe" for Luke is always a positive expression, an expression of victory as the church moved forward in its growth and numbers. Those who "believe" enjoy genuine Christian status. "Believe" is *never* used with a duplicitous, false, or ironic sense. So, not surprisingly, the belief that Jesus talked about in the parable of the sower is conjoined with being saved in Luke 8:12. It is *saving* belief! And yet this seed eventually fell away.

Some have interpreted Simon Magus' act of believing in Acts 8:12,13 as insincere and false, since he and Peter confronted each other later in the chapter. Not only does Luke's use of "belief" elsewhere in Luke and Acts render such a conclusion unlikely, but so also does the immediate context. Simon Magus "believed" in Acts 8:12,13, *even as* the Samaritans believed when they heard the message. Simon Magus was baptized, *even as* the Samaritans were baptized. The acts are described in tandem (as John the Baptist and Jesus were described in parallel fashion in Luke 1 and 2). Since the Samaritans received the Word of God with joy in Acts 8:8, the genuineness of Simon Magus' belief should not be doubted. Simon Magus is an instance of a person who "believed and was baptized" (verse 13) but fell away from his initial faith. He is a vivid example of what Jesus talked about in Luke 8 regarding the seed that fell on the rocky soil. He fell prey to the devil's temptations. Where one demon was cast out, seven more returned (Luke 11:25-27).[4]

With Simon Magus, Luke describes a Christian believer who fell away from his faith. "Once saved, always saved" is simply not biblical. As the seed that fell on the good soil shows, Christian believers must persevere in their faith to the end. In this regard, Luke is not alone. The author of Hebrews repeatedly warns his audience to persevere lest they fall away from the faith. In Hebrews 2:1-3, it states:

> We must pay more careful attention, therefore, to what we have heard, so that we do not drift away. For if the message spoken by angels was binding, and every violation and disobedience received its just punishment, how shall we escape if we ignore such a great salvation?

In Hebrews 3:18–4:1,11, the author is concerned that his hearers do not become like the wilderness generation that provoked God's judgment:

> And to whom did God swear that they would never enter his rest if not to those who disobeyed? So we see that they were not able to enter, because of their unbelief. Therefore, since the promise of entering his rest still stands, let us be careful that none of you be found to have fallen short of it. . . . Let us, therefore, make every effort to enter that rest, so that no one will fall by following their example of disobedience.

In Hebrews 12:25, the author warns of turning away: "See to it that you do not refuse him who speaks. If they did not escape when they refused him who warned them on earth, how much less will we, if we turn away from him who warns us from heaven?" These passages form a pattern: 1. The *subject* committing or in danger of committing sin; 2. the *sin;* 3. the *exhortation* to persevere; 4. the *consequences* of that sin and falling away.[5]

In Hebrews 6:4-6, another instance of this pattern, the main clause reads: "It is impossible . . . to be brought back to repentance." This clause is then modified by several other clauses that describe those who may not be restored. They "have once been enlightened." They "have

132

tasted the heavenly gift." They "have shared in the Holy Spirit." They "have tasted the goodness of the word of God and the powers of the coming age," and yet "they fall away." Two clauses then explain why these people cannot be renewed to repentance. "They are crucifying the Son of God all over again and subjecting him to public disgrace." The positive language in these verses describes *Christians* elsewhere in Hebrews and the New Testament. Hebrews 10:32 employs "received the light" (enlightened) for the converted (see also Luke 11:36; John 1:9; Ephesians 1:18; 3:9). "Taste" in Hebrews 2:9 and 6:4,5 figuratively means "to come to know something or experience it" (so also 1 Peter 2:3). The Hebrews 6 person has, therefore, "tasted" the "heavenly gift" and the "goodness of the word of God and the powers of the coming age." This language parallels Hebrews 3:1: "Holy brothers, who share in the heavenly calling." Hebrews 6:4 also uses the phrase "who have shared in the Holy Spirit." "Share" is never used in Greek literature in the sense of a partial experience. One "shares" in the "heavenly calling" (3:1), in "Christ" (3:14), in the "Holy Spirit" (6:4), and in the Lord's "discipline" (12:8). For the phrase "goodness of the word of God," see "Word" as used in 1:3; 11:3; 12:19. The "powers of the coming age" could refer to the Hebrews' experience of the Spirit's gifts and miracles (2:3,4), or repentance (6:6), or faith (4:3). The author, therefore, is warning genuine Christians against falling away.

Christians are being warned throughout Hebrews. That is why the author regularly includes himself in the warnings. The warnings employ the first person (2:1-4; 3:14; 4:1,11,14-16; 6:1; 10:19; 12:1-3,25-29). The exhorted are the author's "brothers" (3:1,12; 10:19; 13:22), "holy brothers, who share in the heavenly calling" (3:1). The readers are believers whom Christ has saved (2:11,12,17; 4:3). Sometimes the author warns the congregation more directly with the second person pronoun. Those who are in danger of defiling the blood of the covenant (Christ's blood) are the "sanctified," a term used throughout Hebrews for believers. In 2:3,4, the author describes the people's *conversion:* They heard the message of the Lord and experienced miracles and even the gifts of the Spirit. In 6:4-6, they were enlightened, tasted the goodness of God's Word, and experienced the powers of the age to come. They even repented (6:4-6). These are the people who must guard against falling away.

The consequences of falling are indeed serious. The warning passages in Hebrews use dire language, such as: "how shall we escape" (2:3); "angry" (3:10,17); not entering or falling short (3:11,18,19; 4:1,6,11); "fell in the desert" (3:17); "it is impossible . . . to be brought back to repentance" (6:4-6; 12:16,17); "no sacrifice for sins is left" (10:26); "a fearful expectation of judgment and of raging fire that will consume the enemies of God" (10:27); "fire" (10:27; 12:29); "died without mercy" (10:28); punishment/vengeance/retribution (10:29); destruction (10:39). In each of these passages, the author warns his readers about the consequence of *permanent judgment* if they fail to heed his exhortations to avoid sin and to persevere. Hebrews 10:26-31 and 5:11–6:12 offer a blessing for perseverance and a curse for disobedience (see 6:7,8). The placement of the word "impossible" at the beginning of 6:4-6 indicates that the judgment spoken of here is decisive. The hearers must persevere in their good deeds and in faith.

Those adhering to the "once saved, always saved" approach point to passages such as Romans 8:39, "[Nothing can] separate us from the love of God that is in Christ Jesus our Lord." This is one of several passages that explains a Christian's election by God (see also Romans 9 and Ephesians 1). But does this passage really mean that no one can fall away from faith? Paul is assuring his readers in Romans 8 that the powerful, hostile, cosmic forces that oppose God's saving power will not prevail. Similarly, the Evangelist John warns of false shepherds in John 10:28,29 as an *active* evil that snatches away. Paul is not denying an individual's own choice to depart from the faith. While an individual cannot by his or her own power make a decision to be saved, God permits individuals to remove themselves from the ranks of his people. The apostle, therefore, senses a problem emerging even as he claims that nothing can separate us from God's love in Christ. Since Christians are God's elect people, the apostle is forced to digress about another elect people, the Jews (see Romans 9:1-5). How can Christians take comfort in their election when God's election of another people was apparently to no avail? Paul answers in Romans 9:30–10:21 that many of the Jews chose to abandon their God and Messiah. In other words, God's election is always manifested and sure "in Christ." With eyes on ourselves and our frailty, the Scriptures must warn us against falling away and redirect our eyes back to the cross. The certainty of our election is always in the cross. It is no accident that passages about the comfort and certainty of God's election in Christ far outnumber the passages about falling away. The comfort of election is always in the focus on the God who loves us and gives us the strength to persevere.

Paul always says in Romans that God's salvation takes place *in the future,* at the very end of this present age. He always uses the future tense for the verb expressing salvation (see, for instance, Romans 5:9,10; 9:27; 10:9,13; 11:26). The one time he departs from that pattern, in Romans 8:24, he still qualifies salvation with "hope." Ironically, the "once saved, always saved" concept (note the past tense) misinterprets one of its own favorite proof texts and proves itself unbiblical. So often, sinful people—as we all are—interject notions of human wisdom into the text. We don't always hear what the Bible itself says. Danger lurks; our false understanding begins to bear fruit; reasoning adults begin to doubt the miracle that God works in the waters of baptism for little babies.

When people begin to oppose Scriptures such as Luke 8, Hebrews 6, or Hebrews 10 by citing apparently contradictory texts such as Romans 8, a very real danger emerges. We must not set aside the clear witness of Scripture because it disagrees with our way of thinking. Our thinking must yield to God's Word. When apparent conflict emerges between passages, the interpreter must redouble his efforts to make sure he is interpreting both passages correctly. Luke 8, Hebrews 6, and Hebrews 10 set forth clear teaching that believers can fall away. Romans 8, upon more careful examination, never contradicts that teaching. Luke 8, Hebrews 6, and Hebrews 10 should be read in connection with a whole series of Scriptural texts that warn Christians against falling away (John 15:1-6; 1 Corinthians 9:24-27; 15:2; Galatians 5:1-12; 5:16–6:10; 2 Peter 1:4-11; Revelation 2,3).

A friend of mine grew up as a Lutheran and eventually became a Baptist minister. As a young man, he painted homes with the principal of his Lutheran school and another leading church member. Their foul language and excessive alcohol bothered him. He began to have questions about the genuineness of their faith. Although we are never to judge a person's heart, some people's works may, admittedly, be very troubling. Christians should live as Christians. In looking at the poor testimony of many adults baptized as infants, the "once saved, always saved" theology often is easier for human understanding. My friend jumped to the conclusion that his church's teachings must be false, and he left the denomination. Such reasoning led him to reject the miracle of baptism itself. God's precious Word is the antidote to the jadedness that sin encourages. We need to go back to what God does in baptism. It is the beginning of something new in our lives. May we all live in a way that honors what God does for us through Christ in the waters of baptism.

5. Baptism by immersion: necessity or option?

In college I was blessed to know many of the Christians on my campus. During my senior year, a man from off-campus began socializing with several of these Christian students and convinced quite a few of them to begin attending his church. Soon I heard that many of these students were getting baptized again. They had been baptized as babies, but the man told them that they had not *really* been baptized. The problem? My friends had been sprinkled as infants. They had not been immersed, and immersion, said the man, is the true and only mode of baptism. Time to do some more research. I soon realized that water is crucial to baptism, but the amount does not matter.[6]

In John 13:4-10:

> So [Jesus] got up from the meal, took off his outer clothing, and wrapped a towel around his waist. After that, he poured water into a basin and began to wash his disciples' feet, drying them with the towel that was wrapped around him. He came to Simon Peter, who said to him, "Lord, are you going to wash my feet?" Jesus replied, "You do not realize now what I am doing, but later you will understand." "No," said Peter, "you shall never wash my feet." Jesus answered, "Unless I wash you, you have no part with me." "Then, Lord," Simon Peter replied, "not just my feet but my hands and my head as well!" Jesus answered,

"A person who has had a bath needs only to wash his feet; his whole body is clean. And you are clean, though not every one of you."

Peter wanted an immersion, but Jesus responded that a simple washing would do. The mere application of water will suffice, not its quantity. Full immersion is not essential. The *Didache* was written in the late first century, within a generation of the apostles. This manual for Christian worship and living enjoined baptism by means of pouring water over the head three times (7.3). Running water was a preference, but the use of water administered with the triune name was essential.

Most advocates of immersion claim that the Greek word "baptize" must be translated "immerse." The word "baptize" was being used well before the time of the New Testament writers, but to translate the word as "immerse" would be a mistake. For instance, the Greek author Strabo, who lived in the time of Christ, described the exploits of Alexander's army (*Geographica* 14.3.9): "Alexander, meeting with a stormy season, and being a man who in general trusted to luck, set out before the waves had receded; and the result was that all day long his soldiers marched in water submerged [baptized] to their navels" (Jones, LCL). In a similar passage, Polybius in the late third and early second centuries before Christ (*Histories* 3.72.4) described an army crossing waters: "The infantry had great difficulty in crossing, as the water was [lit. being baptized] breast-high" (Paton, LCL). Whereas many contexts remain ambiguous on whether the "baptized" individuals were immersed, in several instances, as in Strabo or Polybius, the context is clear that the "baptism" was not an immersion.

The Greek word "baptize" was an interesting choice on the part of the Jewish people and the New Testament authors. Ancient authors used the word "baptize" *(baptizo)* for an application of liquid that in some way *influenced* the recipient. So the soldiers in the above examples were able to pass through the water only with difficulty. The flowing waters hindered their movement. Likewise, one could be "baptized" with wine, as dinnertime would-be philosophers were described by Athenaeus in the fourth century B.C. (5.64): "You seem to me, O connivalists! to be flooded, beyond expectation, with impetuous words, and to be mersed [baptized] by unmixed wine."[7] Here the liquid influenced the individual by its intoxicating effects. So also Plutarch, a near contemporary of Paul, wrote in his *Causes of Natural Phenomena (Moralia* 914D): "Why do people pour sea-water into wine (and it is said that the men . . . had an oracle directing them to dip *[baptizo]* Dionysus in the sea)?" (Pearson and Sandbach, LCL). The wine there was mixed with water to temper its controlling influence. The early first century Jewish philosopher Philo of Alexandria in his "On the Contemplative Life" (46) described some who were *slightly intoxicate*d on their way to becoming *thoroughly drunk [baptisthenai].* The Greek *"baptizo"* was also used for washings that had a purifying effect or influence. For instance, the late first century Jewish historian Josephus used the verb "baptize" to describe sprinkling a purifying mixture of water and ashes *(Ant.* 4.4.6 §81). The Greek word "baptize" could also be used in connection with full immersion, since the object (often a ship) or person was enveloped and covered by the waters. The ship was sunk. The person could have drowned under the water's influence. How appropriate, then, that the biblical writers chose *"baptizo,"* a word that conveys no mere washing but an application of a liquid that influences the individual. What is the influencing agent of water baptism? The Holy Spirit!

The early church fathers interpreted various Old Testament sprinklings in terms of water baptism. For them, baptism signified not a mode but rather an influence. For instance, Ezekiel 36:25,26 prophesied God's sprinkling of clean water upon the people and the granting of the Spirit. The fourth century Christian father Jerome commented on Ezekiel: "And I will pour out (or sprinkle) upon you clean water . . . so that upon the believing and those converted, I will pour out the clean water of saving baptism, and I will cleanse them from their abominations and from all their errors, with which they have been possessed, and I will give to them a new heart, that they may believe upon the Son of God, and a new spirit."[8] For Jerome, water baptism could be administered in the same manner of pouring or sprinkling as in the prophecy of Ezekiel. The late second-century Christian scholar Clement of Alexandria (2.649; see also Jerome, *Homily* 76) even referred to baptizing by tears.

In Mark 7:1-4:

> The Pharisees and some of the teachers of the law who had come from Jerusalem gathered around Jesus and saw some of his disciples eating food with hands that were "unclean"—that is, ceremonially unwashed *[aniptos]*—hands. (The Pharisees and all the Jews do not eat unless they give their hands a ceremonial washing *[nipto]*, holding to the tradition of the elders. When they come from the marketplace they do not eat unless they wash. And they observe many other traditions, such as the washing *[baptizo]* of cups, pitchers and kettles.)

A variant reading of Mark 7:4 began to circulate in the textual tradition, and the Greek-speaking scribes who copied Mark's Gospel did not object. Many very early manuscripts of Mark included "dining couches" among those items baptized by the Jews before each meal. Such a ceremonial cleaning of the dining couch prior to each meal would have been by means of an ordinary washing, not an immersion. Native Greek speakers labeled the action *"baptizo."* The image of entire couches immersed before a meal is rather bizarre. "Wash" and "baptize" were often used interchangeably. While the Jews washed *(nipto)* their hands before meals according to Mark 7:2,3 (so also Matthew 15:2), Luke 11:37,38 described that activity as *"baptizo."* In 2 Kings 3:11, the servant poured water on the master's hands to wash them before the meal. "Baptize" may therefore be used for the application of water to a body part. In his commentary, the second-century B.C. Greek-speaking author of the apocryphal Ecclesiasticus (34:30 [34:25 LXX]) labeled the "sprinkling" of water and ashes in Numbers 19:17,18 an act of baptizing *(baptizo)*. In the Septuagintal Greek translation of the original Hebrew text of Daniel 4:33, Nebuchadnezzar's body was drenched *[bapto]* with the dew that fell on him from heaven.

Hebrews 9:10 refers to "various ceremonial washings" that the author lists as types of "baptisms" *(diaphorois baptismois)*. Included among these baptismal acts in verse 13 is the sprinkling *(rhantizo)* of the heifer's ashes mixed with water to render the recipients ceremonially clean, as in Numbers 19:17,18. Another example is in Hebrews 9:19: "When Moses had proclaimed every commandment of the law to all the people, he took the blood of calves, together with water, scarlet wool and branches of hyssop, and sprinkled *[rhantizo]* the scroll and all the people" (cf. Exodus 24:6,8). Another instance of baptism by sprinkling is in Hebrews 9:21: "In the same way, he sprinkled *[rhantizo]* with the blood both the tabernacle and everything used in its ceremonies" (cf. Leviticus 8:19; 16:14). That the Greek-speaking author of Hebrews felt comfortable including various ceremonial acts of sprinkling as types of "baptism" demonstrates that the Greek word does not mean "immerse."

The Greek verb *"baptizo"* is not the only instance where those predisposed toward immersion force particular translations of the ancient text to favor their position. With Jesus' baptism by John, immersionists prefer the translation that Jesus was baptized "in" *(en)* the Jordan River (Matthew 3:6; Mark 1:5,9). An equally acceptable translation of the Greek *"en"* would have Jesus baptized "at" the Jordan River, that is, in the general location of the Jordan River. In Mark 1:10 the immersionist emphasizes that Jesus "was coming up out of" *(ek),* but the Greek preposition may just as well be translated "[Jesus] went up *from*" with no implication as to the baptismal mode. The verse may merely express movement or geography. The likelihood that the Synoptic Gospels of Matthew, Mark, and Luke are referring to geography (the Jordan River area) and not a mode (immersion *in* the Jordan River) is strengthened by the explanation in John's Gospel. Scholars recognize that the Fourth Gospel frequently elaborates on the historical material the other three Gospel writers drew upon and corrects some (already) popular misunderstandings. John the Evangelist explains that John the Baptist was actually baptizing not at the Jordan River itself but at "Bethany *on the other side of* [lit. beyond] the Jordan" (John 1:28). John's Gospel corrects any misimpression that the Baptist was baptizing in the Jordan River.

John adds that the Baptist was also baptizing at Aenon near Salim because (according to the New International Version) "there was plenty of water" there (3:23). The NIV actually mistranslates the Greek. *"Hudata polla"* literally means "many waters." Indeed, the name "Aenon" in Aramaic is a contraction of a word

142

that means "springs." The third century A.D. church historian Eusebius in his *Onomasticon* (40) located Aenon 8 Roman miles south of Betshan at the site of five natural springs. The largest was called Ed-Der. "Many waters" makes perfect sense as a reference to these springs. The preference for ritual washings in spring water is based on Leviticus 14, which repeatedly mentions fresh, purifying, running water. The quantity of water is not an issue. By "many waters," John refers to the springs in this area and not to the quantity of water necessary for immersion.

According to Luke, Philip encountered an Ethiopian eunuch reading the Scriptures on a "desert road" (Acts 8:26). Water would have been scarce in an area of desert-like conditions. Desert conditions would explain why, after Philip's interpreting the Scriptures, the eunuch interjected, "Lo, water." The "lo," or "behold," likely conveys a sense of surprise at finding water in that particular location. The amount of water is conveyed by the Greek word *"ti,"* meaning "some." They came across *"some* water," not a large quantity. Luke explains that they came *"upon* some water" *(epi ti hudor),* at which point Philip and the eunuch "stepped down" from the chariot into the water. They did not dismount and then subsequently proceed into the water. The Greek word *"katabaino"* is regularly used for stepping down. In Matthew 14:29 (literally translated), "Peter having *stepped down (katabas)* from the boat walked upon the water *(epi ta hudata)*." Peter's subsequent walking on the water is expressed by a word *other* than the word used for stepping down. Judges 4:15 in the Septuagint reads, "And Sisera stepped down *(katebe)* from his chariot." Since the eunuch stepped down from the chariot right into the water, the water would have been shallow. After the baptism, Philip and the eunuch, of course, "came up" *(anebesan),* or stepped up out of the water. Josephus (*Ant.* 12.4.3 §172) used the same word to express mounting or stepping up into a chariot, as did also the classical Greek authors Herodotus, Homer, Plato, and Xenophon. As "*katabaino*" brought them down from the chariot, so "*anabaino*" took them back up into it. The eunuch's chariot was either on the water or immediately adjacent to it. The New Testament nowhere describes a baptism by immersion.

For immersionists, Romans 6:3-5 portrays immersion and emersion as a sort of burial in and rising again from the waters. Although this interpretation has enjoyed great popularity in evangelical circles, Paul employs a Greek prepositional construction that stresses the *means* by which individuals are buried with Christ, not location (*dia* + genitive; not *en*). Paul also uses a "*sun-*" compound verb *(sunetaphemen)* for being buried *with* Christ. The Christian is "united" to Christ (verse 5, *sumphutoi;* yet another "*sun-*" compound). In baptism, the believer is united to and *participates in* Christ's death and burial (verse 6, *sunestaurothe*). Similarly, baptism takes the individual not "into" water, as if a particular mode were at issue, but rather "into" *(eis)* Christ's death. To be "baptized . . . into *(eis)* one body" in 1 Corinthians 12:13 is to be incorporated into that reality. Those "baptized into" Christ in Galatians 3:27-29 have "clothed [themselves] with" Christ.[9] In Romans 6:3-5, since the baptized have been incorporated into Christ's death, they have the assurance of rising again at the Last Day. Paul makes no reference to the mode of baptism in these verses. The apostle is concerned exclusively with the powerful change that takes place in the baptismal waters. One searches in vain to find a confirming New Testament passage where the physical movements of immersion and emersion are granted symbolical significance.

Figure 1

Figure 2

The earliest depiction of Jesus' baptism comes from a fresco in the Crypt of Lucina from A.D. 100, shortly after the Apostles' own generation (Figure 1).[10] John the Baptist appears clothed and standing on dry ground. From the position of the Baptist on the ground, Jesus is in water no higher than his knees. In a fresco from the Gallery of the Sacraments in S. Callistus that dates to A.D. 200, the Baptist is again on dry ground and Jesus is in ankle-deep water (Figure 2). The Baptist has his hand on the head of the baptized Jesus (portrayed as a small boy). Another fresco from the same time and location once again places Jesus in ankle-deep water as the Baptist pours water over Jesus' head (Figure 3). A fresco from A.D. 250 in the Cemetery of

Figure 3

Saints Petrus and Marcellinus has John the Baptist on dry ground with his right hand on Christ's head. The water around Jesus is ankle-deep (Figure 4). The ankle-deep water in the very first frescoes betrays the lack of emphasis by the earliest Christian artists on any need for immersion. A very late second-century fresco from the Cemetery of Praetestatus depicts a fully clothed individual with the administrant holding a cane

Figure 4

145

Figure 5

over the baptized's head (Figure 5). The clothing and orientation toward the head argue against immersion. Other third century, pre-Constantinian frescoes depict baptism through images of falling water (Figures 6 and 7). Several immediately post-Constantinian frescoes depict water falling on people's heads, the administrant's hand over the baptized's head, or ordinary clothing during the baptism. Such details reinforce the impression that water was poured over the baptized.

Many Christians have been baptized as infants or adults by means of water sprinkled or poured over their

Figure 6

Figure 7

heads. That anyone would be led to doubt his or her baptism is utterly tragic. The meaning of the Greek word "baptize," the New Testament examples of baptism, and the testimony of the first Christians should give comfort to those who were baptized by means of water poured or sprinkled over their heads. Water applied in the name of the triune God—whether to an adult, a child, or an infant—conveys divine power by God's Spirit. Baptism conveys the assurance and comfort of Christ's forgiveness.

NOTES

1. BAPTISM AND ORIGINAL SIN

1. Francis Pieper, *Christian Dogmatics*, Vol. I (St. Louis: Concordia Publishing House, 1950), p.539.
2. Saarnivaara, *Scriptural Baptism*, p.45.
3. In John 3:5 Christ uses the "aorist" passive subjunctive which literally means "once-born". Only one preposition (ex) appears in the Greek. This makes "and" (kai) a coordinating conjunction.
4. Frederick Dale Bruner, *A Theology of the Holy Spirit* (Grand Rapids: William B. Eerdmans Publishing Co., 1970), p.258.
5. Bruner, p.258.

2. BAPTISM FOR SALVATION AND FORGIVENESS OF SINS

1. See again Chapter 1.
2. Francis Pieper, *Christian Dogmatics* Vol. III (St. Louis: Concordia Publishing House, 1953), p.268.
3. Walter Bauer, William F. Arndt, and F. Wilbur Gingrich write in their leading koine Greek lexicon that "eis" here in Acts 2:38 is "to denote purpose . . . eis aphesin hamartion *for the forgiveness of sins, so that sins might be forgiven.* Mt 26:28; cf. Mk 1:4; Luke 3:3; Acts 2:38." *A Greek-English Lexicon of the New Testament and Other Early Christian Literature* (Chicago: Univ. of Chicago Press, 1957), p.228. On the use of the second person imperative with the third person imperative, see Carroll D. Osburn, "The Third Person Imperative in Acts 2:38," *Restoration Quarterly* 26 (1983):81-84. This is an idiomatic usage that functions distributively. Not a single person is exempt. J.C. Davis shows that the *eis* is purposive (*"for* the forgiveness of sins") and *not* casual

("because of the forgiveness of sins"). Note the very important parallel in Matthew 26:28: "For this is my blood of the covenant, which is poured out *for* many *for* [and *not* "because"] the forgiveness of sins." The grammars and lexicons agree Acts 2:38 is *"for* the forgiveness of sins." See J.C. Davis, "Another Look at the Relationship Between Baptism and Forgiveness of Sins in Acts 2:38," *Restoration Quarterly* 24 (1981):80-88. Again, this understanding is demanded by the context.

4. Saarnivaara, *Scriptural Baptism*, p.31.

5. Martin Luther, *Luther's Small Catechism* (Milwaukee: Northwestern Publishing House, 1982), p. 233.

6. W. F. Flemington, *The New Testament Doctrine of Baptism* (London: S.P.C.K., 1964), pp.146-147.

7. Saarnivaara writes (p.39): "In ordinary speech, and according to ordinary grammar, the preposition 'through' or 'by' (in Greek *'dia'* with genitive) denotes means, instrument, way, channel, and so forth. The dictionaries explain that 'through' means 'by way of,' 'by means of,' 'by the instrumentality or aid of.' The preposition 'by' means 'through the agency, means or help of.'"

8. Oscar Cullman, *Baptism in the New Testament* (Philadelphia: Westminster Press, 1950), p.15.

9. See the discussion of Ephesians 5:25-27 a few paragraphs later where the use of the verb in "you have washed" is discussed.

10. Review Chapter 1 on John 3:6-8, especially the connection between baptism and the work of the Spirit.

11. Instrumental dative.

12. Acts 2:38; Acts 8:14-17; Acts 9:18; Acts 8:38-39; Acts 10:44-48; and *Acts 11:15-16* and Acts 19:5-6. F.D. Bruner develops this point in some detail. See his *A Theology of the Holy Spirit* (Grand Rapids: William B. Eerdmans Publishing, 1970), pp.155-218.

13. Again, review Chapter 1 on this passage.

14. Joachim Jeremias, *Infant Baptism in the First Four Centuries* (Philadelphia: Westminster Press, 1962), p.47.

15. Jeremias, *Infant*, pp.47-48.

16. R. C. H. Lenski, *The Interpretation of I and II Corinthians* (Minneapolis: Augsburg Publishing House, 1963), pp.689-690.

3. INFANT FAITH AND BAPTISM (PART I)

1. Karl Barth, *Church Dogmatics* (Edinburgh: T & T Clark, 1969), pp.165-166.

2. Theodore G. Tappert (trans. and ed.), *The Book of Concord* (Philadelphia: Fortress Press, 1959), p.443.

3. Martin Luther, *What Luther Says*, Vol. I, compiled by Ewald M. Plass (St. Louis: Concordia Publishing House, 1959), p.53.
4. David Scaer (p.36) writes:
   People who do not accept infant faith say that children do not know what they are doing, because perhaps they are not in a state of consciousness. But this quality of being self-directed and self-concerned which counts very highly in this world is considered anything but a virtue by Jesus. This child is great in faith, because he is concerned not about his faith but only about grace.
5. Scaer, Chapter 5 Notes. See also: Joseph Henry Thayer, *The New Thayer's Greek-English Lexicon of the New Testament* (Peabody, MA: Hendrickson Publishers, 1981), p.414; Walter Bauer, William Arndt, and F. Wilbur Gingrich, *A Greek-English Lexicon of the New Testament and Other Early Christian Literature* (Chicago: University of Chicago Press, 1957), p.523.
6. James Strong, *A Concise Dictionary of the Words of the New Testament* (Nashville: Abingdon, 1980), p.58. See also: Bauer, Arndt, and Gingrich, pp.665-667; Thayer, pp.511-512. This word is used also in John 6:35; 6:47; 11:26; 12:46; Rom. 9:33; 10:11; Mark 15:32; etc.
7. Some have attempted to exclude infants from the kingdom of heaven by saying "such as these" excludes the infants referred to. But this is grammatically invalid. For example, Matthew 9:8 uses the same construction: "When the crowds saw it, they were afraid, and they glorified God, who had give *such authority* to men." Was not "such authority" a reference to authority even as and *including* that which had just been demonstrated? So infants would be included among those to whom the kingdom of heaven belongs.
8. Gottfried Hoffman, "The Baptism and Faith of Children," *A Lively Legacy*, eds. Kurt E. Marquart, John R. Stephenson, and Bjarne W. Teigen (Fort Wayne: Concordia Theological Seminary Press, 1985), p.85.
9. Some have said that "like a little child" excludes the little child and that this applies *only* to those adults who have become like little children. But adults receive the kingdom *as a little child receives the kingdom*! That children receive the kingdom and so are saved is necessary to understand the point regarding adults' reception of the kingdom.
10. See also Jeremiah 1:5; Galatians 1:15; Luke 1:15.

4. INFANT FAITH AND BAPTISM (PART II)

1. Saarnivaara, *Scriptural Baptism*, pp.55-56.
2. Saarnivaara, *Scriptural Baptism*, p.56.
3. See Section 4.
4. Suggestion: It is possible that Chapters 1 and 2 were read with various objections to infant faith constantly coming to mind that were later answered. Therefore a rereading of Chapters 1 and 2, keeping in mind this section, may be helpful. Baptism is the means entrusted to the Church by which infants are saved from damnation, for infants receive freely the grace offered them by Scriptures in baptism.
5. Hoffman, p.92.
6. Cullman, pp.53-54.
7. Compare the text of his response to the text of the blind man's response to healing in John 9. Culpepper (pp.140-141) notes the following similarities:
   (1) Both men's history is described (5:5; 9:1).
   (2) Jesus takes the initiative to heal both (5:6; 9:6).
   (3) A body of water is described as having healing power in John 5, and in 9:7 the blind man is healed at the pool of Siloam (9:7).
   (4) Jesus heals on the sabbath (5:9; 9:14).
   (5) Jews charge Jesus with breaking the sabbath (5:10; 9:16).
   (6) Jews ask who healed the individual (5:12; 9:15).
   (7) The men do not know where Jesus is (5:13; 9:12).
   (8) Jesus finds them and invites belief (5:14; 9:35).
   (9) The connection between sin and suffering is explored (5:14; 9:35).
   (10) The one goes to the Jews (5:15) while the other is cast out by the Jews (9:34,35).
   (11) Jesus must work as the Father is working (5:17; 9:4). Culpepper explains that by these similarities the blind man in John 9 serves as a "counterpart" and "contrast" to the lame man in John 5 (p.141). John sets up the parallel with all the similarities. But then comes the major difference. While the blind man came to see who Jesus was and confessed Jesus Christ to the Jews, the lame man never recognized the Christ and ended up reporting him to the hostile Jewish authorities. In John's strictly dualistic framework (recall the discussion in chapter 1 of John's dualism), while the one came to faith, the other never came to believe. Jesus physically healed a man who had never

entered into a belief in Jesus Christ as the only-begotten of the Father.

8. Infant blessing is also known as infant "dedication" or "christening."
9. See Chapter 5.
10. We saw that in passage after passage in Chapter 2.
11. Hoffman, pp.80-81.
12. See Chapter 2.
13. Cullman, p.73.
14. Cullman, p.74.
15. The irregular infinitive construction of "koluein."
16. Cullman, pp.78-79.
17. Jeremias, *Infant*, p.50.
18. Jeremias, *Infant*, pp.51-53.
19. Jeremias found the peculiar use of the word *koluein* with Baptism also in the the early Church's *Pseudo-Clementine Homilies* "What *hinders* me from being baptized today?" (13.5.1) and "Now, nothing hinders her from being baptized" (13.11.2). In the Syriac version of the early Irene legend, this use of "*koluein*" with baptism is found.
20. See Chapter 8.
21. Jeremias, *Infant*, p.54.

5. CHRIST'S COMMAND IN MATTHEW 28:18-20

1. Karl Barth, *Church Dogmatics*, Vol.4, Part 4, G. W. Bromiley and T.F. Torrance (eds.) (Edinburgh: T & T Clark, 1969), p.179.
2. H.N. Ridderbos, *Matthew*, trans. by Ray Togtman (Grand Rapids: Zondervan Publishing House, 1987), p.12. See also: Jack Dean Kingsbury, *Matthew as Story*, Second Ed. (Philadelphia: Fortress Press, 1988), pp.149-150.
3. Ridderbos, p.12.
4. David P. Scaer, *Life, New Life and Baptism* (Fort Wayne: Concordia Theological Seminary), p.20. See also Luke 18:15's parallel description.
5. Scaer, p.20.
6. Scaer, p.21. As if to reinforce the point, Matthew juxtaposes Christ's talk with the rich young man with his rebuke of the disciples for trying to keep the children away. The disciples seemed to have doubts about small children's ability to receive the things of the kingdom of heaven. But the Lord says "of such" is the kingdom of heaven (19:14). The rich man, however, was a different matter. Surely an adult man who had done his best to

obey the commandments would be a better candidate for the kingdom of heaven than the small child. But unlike what Jesus says of the children, he says of the rich man that "it's easier for a camel to go through the eye of a needle than for a rich man to enter the kingdom of God" (19:24). For "it will be hard for a rich man to enter the kingdom of God" (19:23). The disciples ask: "Who then can be saved?" Jesus explains that with men this is impossible but with God all things are possible.

Jesus totally reverses the disciples' preconceptions. Where there was doubt about small children, Jesus assures the disciples that such are prime recipients of the kingdom of heaven. But with the rich man, on the other hand, Jesus does the exact reverse. He creates doubt. Salvation is impossible for both the rich man and the infant, but indeed, perhaps more so with the rich man. Scaer points out:

"If it is possible for a rich man who is encumbered with this world's concerns to enter the kingdom, how much easier is it then for children, who are held up as examples."

7. Baptizing is a participle deriving imperatival force from the verb. David J. Hesselgrave, *Planting Churches Cross-Culturally* (Grand Rapids: Baker Book House, 1980), p.23. See also: R. T. France, *Matthew* (Grand Rapids: Wm. B. Eerdmans Publishing Co., 1985), p.414; Robert G. Bratcher, *A Translator's Guide to the Gospel of Matthew* (London: United Bible Societies, 1981), p.376; R.C.H. Lenski, *The Interpretation of St. Matthew* (Minneapolis: Augsburg Publishing House, 1961), pp.1172-3.

8. David J. Bosch, "The Structure of Mission: An Exposition of Matthew 28:16-20," *Exploring Church Growth*, Wilbert R. Shenk, ed. (Grand Rapids: William B. Eerdmans Publishing Co., 1983), p.237.

9. Douglas Ehninger and Wayne Brockriede, *Decision by Debate*, Second Ed. (New York: Harper and Row Publishers, 1978), pp.135-136.

10. "Make disciples" (*matheteusate*) is followed by the participles "baptizing" (*baptidsontes*) and "teaching" (*didaskontes*). Hence: "make disciples by baptizing and teaching." Had Jesus meant to say "Having made disciples, baptize and teach" (thereby separating the baptizing from the making disciples of), the imperative "make disciples" would rather have been the participle "having made disciples" (*mathateusantes*). The participles "baptizing" (*baptidsontes*) and "teaching" (*didaskontes*) would have been the imperatives "baptize" (*baptidsete*) and "teach" (*didaskete*). Rather the two modal participles "'baptizing" and "teaching" are

subordinated to "make disciples." See Bosch, pp.230-231; A.T. Robertson, *A Grammar of the Greek New Testament in the Light of Historical Research* (Nashville, TN: Broadman Press, 1934), p.1128; Bratcher, p.376; France, p.414; Lenski, pp.1172-3.

11. See Chapters 3 and 4 on infant faith.
12. Francis Brown, S.R. Driver and Charles A. Briggs, *The New Brown-Driver-Briggs-Gesenius Hebrew and English Lexicon* (Peabody, MA: Hendrickson Publishers, 1979), pp. 881-2. "The Hebrew word for 'least' is 'chatan' which is translated as 'mikros' in the Greek, a term used by Jesus for the youngest children." David P. Scaer, *Life, New Life and Baptism* (Fort Wayne: Concordia Theological Seminary Press), p.49.
13. Cf. Brown-Driver-Briggs, p.882.
14. Ronald J. Williams, *Hebrew Syntax: An Outline*, Second Ed. (Toronto: Univ. of Toronto Press, 1976), pp.54,55,57.
15. C.F. Keil, "Minor Prophets," Part One, *Commentary on the Old Testament*, Vol. X, by C. F. Keil and F. Delitzsch (Grand Rapids: William B. Eerdmans Publishing Co.), p.416.
16. Scaer, p.20. Also, note that ancient censuses included infants.

6. PAUL'S COMPARISON OF CIRCUMCISION AND BAPTISM

1. While the word "covenant" is here being used, "covenant" assumes a two-sided agreement with two responsible parties. However, the word translated as "covenant" is probably better translated as "testament," that which is willed and passed on to the recipient by the death of the testator. J. Barton Payne defends the "testamental" understanding of the word. See especially pp.96-99 in his *Theology of the Older Testament* (Grand Rapids: Zondervan Publishing House, 1962).
2. Uuras Saarnivaara, *Scriptural Baptism* (New York: Vantage Press, 1953), p.5.
3 At this point, the issue of infant faith may come to mind. The unique promise of baptism's creation of faith, most notably infant faith, was discussed in Chapters 2,3 and 4.
4. Oscar Cullman, *Baptism in the New Testament* (Philadelphia: Westminster Press, 1950), p.57.
5. William F. Arndt and F. Wilbur Gingrich, *A Greek-English Lexicon of the New Testament and Other Early Christian Literature* (Chicago: University of Chicago Press, 1957), p.804.
6. Cullman, p.61.
7. A topic to be more thoroughly explored in Chapter 7.

8. Geoffrey W. Bromiley, *Children of Promise* (Grand Rapids: Wm. B. Eerdmans, 1979), p.21.
9. See also Gal. 6:12,13 and 5:2,3. J. Barton Payne's discussion in *The Theology of Older Testament*, pp.393-394 is also helpful here.
10. See Chapter 7.

7. JEWISH BAPTISMAL CUSTOMS AT THE TIME OF CHRIST

1. Alfred Edersheim, *The Life and Times of Jesus the Messiah* Part One (Grand Rapids: William B. Eerdmans Publishing Co., 1971), p.747.
2. See Pesahim 8:8 and Eduyoth 5:2 in *The Mishnah*, trans. Herbert Danby (London: Oxford University Press, 1938), pp.148,431.
3. S.M. Merrill, *Christian Baptism: Its Subjects and Mode* (Cincinnati: Cranston and Stowe, 1876), pp.121-136.
4. As quoted in Joachim Jeremias, *Infant Baptism in the First Four Centuries* (Philadelphia: Westminster Press, 1962), p.26.
5. Jeremias, *Infant,* p.27.
6. Jeremias, *Infant,* p.27.
7. "In fact nearly all scholars in the last sixty years who have concerned themselves with the date of the introduction of proselyte baptism have come to the conclusion that it came into practice in pre-Christian times," Jeremias, pp.28-29. That the Jews would begin such a practice after Christ would seem inconceivable. Why would the Jews imitate a Christian practice given their hatred for the Christians? Surely someone would have disputed the adoption of a Christian practice into Judaism, of which dispute we would have some knowledge.
8. Jeremias, *Infant,* pp.37-39.
9. W.F. Flemington, *The New Testament Doctrine of Baptism* (London: William Clowes and Sons, Ltd., 1948), p.131; cf. *Bab. Ketuboth lla.*
10. Jeremias, *Infant,* pp.32-36; William G. Braude, *Jewish Proselytizing* (Providence, RI: Brown University Press, 1940), p.74.
11. John 3:3-10 represents a "rabbinic" dialogue. All throughout John's Gospel, Jesus is presented as the true rabbi whose teacher was the Father himself as opposed to the Jewish rabbis whose teachers are men. This motif picks up again in John 3:3-10 as Nicodemus and Jesus are referred to as "teachers" and "rabbis." Jesus then speaks in terms of what "we" know as opposed to Nicodemus and his authorities. In verse 7 "do not be surprised"

was a typical rabbinic phrase (see: Rudolph Bultmann's *The Gospel of John*, Westminster, 1971, p.142, and Raymond Brown's *The Gospel According to John I-XII,* Doubleday, 1966, p.LXIf).

This is very significant in terms of the baptismal discussion in these verses. The Jews spoke of their converts as "born again" in their baptism. But, not all the rabbis were agreed on the benefits of convert baptism. Could it be that when Jesus speaks of being "born again," Nicodemus responded with a standard response he used against his own peers who advocated baptism as a means of being "born again" into Judaism? "How can a man enter back into his mother's womb to be born again?" If this understanding of the rabbinic debate in John 3:3-8 is correct, this is further evidence for the Jewish convert baptism before Christ.

12. Uuras Saarnivaara, *Can the Bible Be Trusted* (Minneapolis, MN: Osterhus Publishing House, 1983), p.202.

8. THE BAPTISM OF ENTIRE FAMILIES AND HOUSEHOLDS

1. Mary Johnston, *Roman Life* (Chicago: Scott, Foresman and Co., 1957), p.105.
2. Frank Gardner Moore, *The Roman's World* (New York: Columbia University Press, 1936), p.183.
3. O.A.W. Dilke, *The Ancient Romans: How They Lived and Worked* (London: David and Charles Publishers Limited, 1975), p.79.
4. William Stearns Davis, *A Day in Old Rome: A Picture of Roman Life* (New York: Allyn and Bacon Publishers, 1925), p.130.
5. Joachim Jeremias, *The Origins of Infant Baptism* (Naperville, IL: Alec R. Allenson, Inc., 1963), pp.17-18.
6. Joachim Jeremias, *The Origins of Infant Baptism* (Naperville, IL: Allen R. Allenson, 1963) p.14.
7. Jeremias, *Infant*, p.20.
8. Jeremias, *Origins*, p.20.
9. Jeremias, *Origins*, p.21.
10. Jeremias, *Origins*, p.20.
11. Henry Wheeler Robinson, *Corporate Personality in Ancient Israel*, Rev. Ed. (Edinburgh: T & T Clark and Fortress Press, 1981), p.26.
12. Jeremias, *Infant*, p.23.
13. See the more complete discussion of these matters in Chapter 9.
14. R. C. H. Lenski, *The Interpretation of the Acts of the Apostles* (Minneapolis: Augsburg Publishing House, 1934), p.661.

15. Samuel J. Baird, *A Bible History of Baptism* (Philadelphia: James H. Baird, 1882), p.472
16. Michael Green, *Evangelism in the Early Church*, p.326 quotes from Vol. 4 of Foakes-Jackson and Kirsopp Lake's (editors) *Beginnings of Christianity*, p.239:
    If the custom of the country was the same as it is now, the period almost exactly covers the time devoted to the midday meal and the siesta. At one p.m. there were probably more people sound asleep than at one a.m.
17. Baird, pp.473-474.
18. Baird, p.474.
19. Baird, p.475.
20. Saarnivaara, p.9.

9. MEMBERS, BY BAPTISM, OF THE FAMILY OF GOD!

1. See Chapter 7.
2. Jeremias, *Origins*, pp. 26-27.
3. Scaer, p. 23.

10. THE TESTIMONY OF THE EARLY CHURCH

1. And circumcision was a rite usually associated with infants. See chapter 6.
2. *Apol. I*,15,6 in *The Ante-Nicene Fathers* (ANF), Vol. I, ed. by Alexander Roberts and James Donaldson (Grand Rapids: Wm. B. Eerdmans Publishing Co., n.d.), p.167. Also, note that Jeremias, in *Origins*, pp.57-8 shows why the phrase "*ek paidon,*" in its context, means "from *infancy*":
    In *Apol. I*,15:1-8, Justin is concerned with sexual discipline (*peri sophrosunes*). In 15.6 and 7f. he adduces, as examples from life, two different groups in the church which he contrasts with each other: the one consists of those who "became disciples of Christ as children" (*ek paidon ematheteuthesan to Christo*) and "remained uncorrupted" up to their old age; the others are "the countless multitude of those who broke away from licentiousness and came to learn this [sexual discipline]" (*to anarithmeton plethos ton ex akolasias metabalonton kai tauta mathonton*). In other words, Justin contrasts those born as Christians with those who became Christians. In the case of the former the value of the evidence for the Christians' superior morality lies in their life-long *sophrosune*; in the case of the latter it depends on the complete change in their manner of life.

Thus, Justin Martyr contrasts those of adult age with those "made disciples" (Matthew 28:19) from earliest childhood, from birth.

3. Flemington writes (p.132):
   "The verb *matheteuo* [make disciples], used here by Justin in the passive, is the same verb that is used transitively in the active in the baptismal passage at the end of Matthew's Gospel [with baptism]."

4. Flemington, p.132.

5. Irenaeus, *Adv. Haer. 3,3,4*. See also Eusebius *Church History* in *The Nicene and Post-Nicene Fathers* (NPNF), Philip Schaff and Henry Wace (ed.), First Series Vol. I (Grand Rapids: Eerdmans Publishing Co., 1952).

6. Jeremias (*Infant*) defends the 167-8 dating at some length against the more accepted 156 A.D. date (pp.60-63). Quasten gives the earlier dating of 156 A.D. See *Patrology*, I, p.77.

7. *Mart. Pol.* 9 in *ANF*, p.41.

8. Jeremias, *Origins*, p.58. Jeremias discusses the evidence from the trip to Anicetus in *Infant*, p.63. Polycrates, in his message to Rome in 190-191 A.D., says that for 65 years he had lived in the Lord. This, again, seems to point to his age at the time of writing and to his infant baptism. See Jeremias, *Infant,* p.63. 122

9. Flemington, p.132.

10. *Adv. Haer.* 2,22,4. See *ANF* I, p.391.

11. Flemington, p.132. Irenaeus uses the phrase *"renascunter in Deum"* in *Adv. Haer.* III,17,1 (*ANF*, I, p.444) and in I,21,1 (*ANF*, I, p.345). The first citation reads: "And then, giving to the disciples the power of regeneration into God, he said to them, 'Go and teach all nations, baptizing them in the name of the Father, and of the Son, and of the Holy Spirit.' Here, the regeneration is explained as baptismal. The second citation speaks of "baptism which is the regeneration to God. . . ." The phrase thus refers to *baptism*.

12. *De Anima* 33:3-40:1, *NPNF* First Series Vol. III, pp.194-195.

13. See Jeremias, *Infant*, pp.84-85.

14. Jeremias, *Infant*, pp.81-85. Also, unmarried persons should be baptized later (because of the temptations they face). So in these convert situations, keep in mind that Tertullian not only questioned infant baptism but also the baptism of certain adults!
    Kurt Aland believes that Tertullian in *De Baptismo* 18 (*ANF* III, p.678) requires that all infants were to baptized later when they were of the age of reason. Assuming Aland is correct and the document was not addressed to the situation of converts, Tertul-

lian still argues in such a way as to show the uniformity and ancient history of the practice (all the stronger as evidence since it would then be coming from an opponent of the practice, the only one of this time-period). First, Tertullian's discussion of the sponsors and their appointed roles in the baptism of infants shows that the rite was well-established. Second, Tertullian recognizes emergency baptisms. This is consistent with what he wrote in *De Anima* 40:1 (*ANF* III, p.220):

"Every soul, then, by reason of its birth, has its nature in Adam until it is born again in Christ, moreover, it is unclean all the while that it remains without this regeneration; and because, it is actively sinful, and suffuses even the flesh (by reason of this conjunction) with its own shame."

It is understandable, in view of this, that Tertullian accepted the emergency baptism of infants. This also clearly attests the custom of the church in baptizing infants. Finally and most decisively, Sasse writes: "When Tertullian in his writing *On Baptism* explicitly opposes the custom of infant baptism, he does not speak against it as though it were an innovation." Hermann Sasse, *We Confess the Sacraments*, trans. Norman Nagel (St. Louis: Concordia Publishing House, 1985), pp.38-39.) See also: *ANF* II, p.678. Certainly if Tertullian wanted to oppose the practice as of more recent origin or only of recent acceptance, he would have said so. This would have powerfully demolished the practice, rather than the weaker and more "torturous" lines of reasoning about godparents dying and the like. But Tertullian's never even hinting at such is the most critical fact in the interpretation of the historical evidence from this period.

This reading of Tertullian is confirmed by the Council in 251-253 only 50 years after Tertullian. The African church reaffirmed infant baptism *unanimously* as the the practice from earliest times. See Cyprian's account in *Epistle* 58 (*ANF* V, pp.353-4). Jeremias summarizes the arguments against Aland's position on the evidence in *Origins*, pp.64-69. While Jeremias' earlier work (*Infant*) and Aland's reply are famous, not as many scholars cite the very important Jeremias reply in *Origins*.

15. Flemington, p.132.
16. E. C. Whitaker, *Documents of the Baptismal Liturgy* (London: SPCK, 1960, 1970), p.5.
17. Jeremias, *Origins*, p.32. And so this practice has continued in many churches to this day.
18. *ANF* V, p.354.
19. Flemington, p.133.

20. As quoted in Johannes Quasten, *Patrology*, Vol. II (Westminster, MD: Christian Classics, 1986), p.83 .

21. Eusebius (*Church History* VI 19.10) says that Origen's family had been Christian. He was carefully taught in all the doctrines of the Christian faith by his father, Leonides, who was then martyred. See *NPNF* First Series Vol. I, p.266. Thus, Jeremias, *Infant*, p.66 writes:

   ". . . he hardly could have spoken of a tradition handed down from the apostles had he not known that at least his father and probably also his grandfather had been baptized as *paidia*."

   With Origen being baptized in A.D. 185, his father would have been baptized in the mid-second century, and his grandfather in the early second century shortly after the apostolic age.

22. Jeremias, *Origins*, p.72.

23. Jeremias, *Infant*, pp.41-42.

24. Jeremias, *Infant*, p.55. "Catechumens" refers to individuals being instructed or "catechized" by the church as converts to the faith.

25. Jeremias, *Infant*, p.75.

26. Jeremias, *Infant,* p.56.

27. Quoted by Augustine, *On Original Sin* II, 20 in *The Nicene and Post-Nicene Fathers*, First Series, Vol. V. Philip Schaff (ed.) (Grand Rapids: Eerdmans, n.d.), p.244.

28. *De Baptismo Contra Donatistas* IV, pp.23-24; translated in William Wall *The History of Infant Baptism*, Vol. 1, pp.254-255.

29. Jeremias, *Infant*, pp.92-93.

30. Jeremias, *Infant*, p.93.

31. Jeremias, *Infant*, p.94.

32. Sasse, p.39.

33. Cullman, p.26.

34. Cullman, p.26.

LINGERING QUESTIONS

1. On the history of the bitter relations between Jews and Samaritans, see especially A. Andrew Das, "Acts 8: Water Baptism and the Spirit," *Concordia Journal* 19 (1993), pp.127-34.

2. Anthony C. Thiselton, *The First Epistle to the Corinthians* (The New International Greek Testament Commentary; Grand Rapids: William B. Eerdmans Publishing Company, 2000), pp.140,142-44.

3. Recent scholarship has confirmed Paul's high view of baptism in 1 Cor 15:29. See the full-length study of Michael F. Hull, *Baptism on Account of the Dead (1 Cor 15:29): An Act of Faith in the*

Resurrection (Academia Biblica 22; Atlanta: Society of Biblical Literature, 2005). First Corinthians 15:29 parallels Paul's claims about baptism in Romans 6 and Galatians 3.

4. For a more thorough discussion of the Acts 8 passage, see A. Andrew Das, "Acts 8: Water Baptism and the Spirit," *Concordia Journal* 19 (1993), pp.108-34.

5. Scot McKnight, "The Warning Passages of Hebrews: A Formal Analysis and Theological Conclusions," *Trinity Journal* 13 (1992), pp. 21-59.

6. See especially James Kerr, *A Treatise on the Mode of Baptism* (Steubenville, OH: Abner L. Frazer, 1844); James W. Dale, *Classic Baptism: An Inquiry into the Meaning of the Word as Determined by the Usage of Classical Greek Writers* (Reprint; Phillipsburg, NJ: Presbyterian and Reformed Publishing, 1989); idem, *Judaic Baptism: An Inquiry into the Meaning of the Word as Determined by the Usage of Classical Greek Writers* (Reprint; Phillipsburg, NJ: Presbyterian and Reformed Publishing, 1991).

7. As cited and discussed by Dale, *Classic Baptism,* p. 319.

8. 5.341-42; as cited and discussed by Dale, *Judaic Baptism,* pp.195-98; note in Dale the similar affirmations of the fulfillment of Ezekiel's prophecy in Christian baptism by other early Christian authors. See the very similar comments in Jerome, *Letter* 69.7 (*NPNF²* 6:146).

9. Robert C. Tannehill, *Dying and Rising With Christ: A Study in Pauline Theology* (BZNW 32; Berlin: Alfred Töpelmann, 1967), pp.22-25.

10. Sketches for Figures 1-7 are reproduced from Clement Francis Rogers, "Baptism and Christian Archaeology," part 4 of vol. 5 of *Studia Biblica et Ecclesiastica* (London: Oxford University Press, 1903), pp.239-58.

BIBLIOGRAPHY

Aland, Kurt. *Did the Early Church Baptize Infants?* G. R. Beasley-Murray (trans.). Philadelphia: Westminster Press, n.d.

Baird, Samuel J. *A Bible History of Baptism.* Philadelphia: James H. Baird, 1882.

Bamherger, Bernard J. *Proselytism in the Talmudic Period.* New York: Ktav Publishing House, 1939.

Barth, Karl. *Church Dogmatics* Vol. IV. Geoffrey W. Bromiley and T. F. Torrance (eds.). Edinburgh: T & T Clark, 1969.

Barth, Karl. *The Teachings of the Church Regarding Baptism.* Ernest A. Payne (trans.). London: S C M Press, 1948.

Bauer, Walter, William F. Arndt, and F. Wilbur Gingrich. *A Greek-English Lexicon of the New Testament and Other Early Christian Literature.* Chicago: University of Chicago Press, 1957.

Bosch, David J. "The Structure of Mission: An Exposition of Matt. 28:16-20." *Exploring Church Growth.* William R. Shenk (ed.). Grand Rapids: William B. Eerdmans Publishing Co., 1983.

Bratcher, Robert G. *A Translator's Guide to the Gospel of Matthew.* London: United Bible Societies, 1981.

Braude, William G. *Jewish Proselytizing.* Providence, RI: Brown University Press, 1940.

Bromiley, Geoffrey W. *Children of Promise.* Grand Rapids: William B. Eerdmans Publishing Co., 1979.

Brown, Francis, S. R. Driver, and Charles A. Briggs. *The New Brown-Driver-Briggs-Gesenius Hebrew and English Lexicon.* Peabody, MA: Hendrikson Publishers, 1979.

Brown, Raymond E. *The Gospel According to John I-XII.* New York: The Anchor Bible (Doubleday), 1966.

Bruner, Frederick Dale. *A Theology of the Holy Spirit.* Grand Rapids: William B. Eerdmans Publishing Co., 1970.

Buchanon, Colin. *A Case For Infant Baptism.* Bramcote, England: Grove Books, 1978.

Buls, Harold. *Notes on Philippians and Colossians.* Fort Wayne: Concordia Theological Seminary Press, 1978.

Bultmann, Rudolf. *The Gospel of John.* G. R. Beasley-Murray, R. W. N. Hoare, and J. K. Riches (trans.). Philadelphia: Westminster Press, 1971.

162

Cullman, Oscar. *Baptism in the New Testament.* J. K. Reid (trans.). Philadelphia: Westminster Press, 1950.

Culpepper, R. Alan. *Anatomy of the Fourth Gospel.* Philadelphia: Fortress Press, 1983.

Danby, Herbert (trans.). *The Mishnah.* London: Oxford University Press, 1938.

Davis, J.C. "Another Look at the Relationship Between Baptism and Forgiveness of Sins in Acts 2:38." *Restoration Quarterly* 24 (1981):80-88.

Davis, William Stearns. *A Day in Old Rome: A Picture of Roman Life.* New York: Allyn and Bacon Publishers, 1925.

Deterding, Paul E. "Baptism According to the Apostle Paul." *Concordia Journal.* Vol. 6 (May 1980).

Dilke, O. A. W. *The Ancient Romans: How They Lived and Worked.* London: David and Charles Publishers, 1975.

Edersheim, Alfred. *The Life and Times of Jesus the Messiah.* Part One. Grand Rapids: William B. Eerdmans Publishing Co., 1971.

Ehninger, Douglas and Wayne Brockriede. *Decision by Debate.* Second Ed. New York: Harper and Row Publishers, 1978.

Engelder, Theodore. *Handbook of Lutheran Theology.* Fort Wayne: Concordia Theological Seminary Press, 1981.

Flemington, W. F. *The New Testament Doctrine of Baptism.* London: S.P.C.K., 1964.

France, R. T. *Matthew.* Grand Rapids: William B. Eerdmans Publishing Co., 1985.

Gonzalez, Justo L. *A History of Christian Thought.* Vol. I. Rev. Ed. Nashville, TN: Abingdon Press, 1970.

Green, Michael. *Evangelism in the Early Church.* Grand Rapids: William B. Eerdmans Publishing Co., 1970.

Hallesby, O. *Infant Baptism and Adult Conversion.* Clarence J. Carleson (trans.). Minneapolis: Augsburg Publishing Co., 1974.

Hesselgrave, David J. *Planting Churches Cross-Culturally.* Grand Rapids: Baker Book House, 1980.

Hoenig, Sidney B. "Conversion During the Talmudic Period." *Conversion to Judaism.* David Max Eichhorn (ed.). New York: Ktav Publishing House, 1965.

Hoffman, Gottfried. "The Baptism and Faith of Children." *A Lively Legacy.* Kurt E. Marquart, John R. Stephenson and Bjarne W. Teigen. Fort Wayne: Concordia Theological Seminary Press, 1985.

Jeremias, Joachim. *Infant Baptism in the First Four Centuries.* David Cairns (trans.). Philadelphia: Westminster Press, 1962.

Jeremias, Joachim. *The Origins of Infant Baptism.* Dorothea M. Barton (trans.). Naperville, IL: Allec R. Allenson, 1963.

Jewett, Paul K. *Infant Baptism and the Covenant of Grace.* Grand Rapids : William B. Eerdmans Publishing Co., 1978.

Johnston, Mary. *Roman Life.* Chicago: Scott, Foresman and Co., 1957.

Jungkuntz, Richard. *The Gospel of Baptism.* St. Louis: Concordia Publishing House, 1968.

Kahane, Howard. *Logic and Philosophy.* Fourth Ed. Chicago: University of Chicago Press, 1957.

Keil, C. F. and F. Delitzsch. *Commentary on the Old Testament in Ten Volumes.* Vols. I and X. Grand Rapids: William B. Eerdmans Publishing Co., n.d.

Kingsbury, Jack Dean. *Matthew as Story.* Second Ed. Philadelphia: Fortress Press, 1988.

Kretzmann, Paul E. *Popular Commentary of the Bible.* Vol. II. St. Louis: Concordia Publishing House, n.d.

Lenski, R. C. H. *The Interpretation of the Acts of the Apostles.* Minneapolis: Augsburg Publishing House, 1934.

Lenski, R. C. H. *The Interpretation of St. Matthew's Gospel.* Minneapolis: Augsburg Publishing Co., 1961.

Lenski, R. C. H. *The Interpretation of St. Paul's Epistles to the Colossians, to the Thessalonicans, to Timothy, to Titus and to Philemon.* Minneapolis: Augsburg Publishing House, 1946.

Lenski, R. C. H. *The Interpretation of I and II Corinthians.* Minneapolis: Augsburg Publishing House, 1963.

Luther, Martin. *Luther's Small Catechism.* St. Louis: Concordia Publishing House, 1943.

Luther, Martin. *What Luther Says.* Vol. I. Ewald M. Plass (compiler). St. Louis: Concordia Publishing House, 1959.

Marshall, Alfred. The *NIV Interlinear Greek-English New Testament.* Grand Rapids: Zondervan Publishing House, 1976.

Merrill, S. M. *Christian Baptism: Its Subjects and Mode.* Cincinnati: Cranston and Stowe, 1876.

Moore, Frank Gardner. *The Roman World.* New York: Columbia University Press, 1936.

Mueller, John Theodore. "Holy Baptism." *The Abiding Word.* St. Louis: Concordia Publishing House, 1947.

Muller, Richard. "Anabaptists and Believer's Baptism." *Ministry* 59 (11):7-9.

Osburn, Carroll D. "The Third Person Imperative in Acts 2:38." *Restoration Quarterly* 26 (1983):81-84.

164

Payne, J. Barton. *The Theology of the Older Testament*. Grand Rapids: Zondervan Publishing House, 1962.

Peters, George W. *A Biblical Theology of Missions*. Chicago: Moody Press, 1972.

Pieper, Francis. *Christian Dogmatics*. Vol. I. St. Louis: Concordia Publishing House, 1950.

Pieper, Francis. *Christian Dogmatics*. Vol. III. St. Louis: Concordia Publishing House, 1953.

Quasten, Johannes. *Patrology*. Vols. I and II. Westminster, MD: Christian Classics, 1986.

Ridderbos, H. N. *Matthew*. Ray Togtman (trans.). Grand Rapids: Zondervan Publishing House, 1987.

Roberts, Alexander and James Donaldson (ed.). *The Ante-Nicene Fathers*, Vols. I, II, V. Grand Rapids: William B. Eerdmans Publishing Co., n.d.

Robertson, A. T. *A Grammar of the Greek New Testament in Light of Historical Research*. Nashville, TN: Broadman Press, 1934.

Robinson, Henry Wheeler. *Corporate Personality in Ancient Israel*. Rev. Ed. Edinburgh: T & T Clark and Fortress Press, 1981.

Saarnivaara, Uuras. *Can the Bible Be Trusted*? Minneapolis: Osterhus Publishing House, 1983.

Saarnivaara, Uuras. *Scriptural Baptism*. New York: Vantage Press, 1953.

Sasse, Hermann. *We Confess the Sacraments*. Norman Nagel (trans.). St. Louis: Concordia Publishing House, 1985.

Scaer, David P. *Life, New Life and Baptism*. Fort Wayne: Concordia Theological Seminary Press, n.d.

Schaff, Philip and Henry Wace (ed.). *The Nicene and Post-Nicene Fathers*, First Series, Vol. I and V. Grand Rapids: William B. Eerdmans Publishing Co., 1952.

Schmied, Heinrich. *The Doctrinal Theology of the Evangelical Lutheran Church*. Third Ed. (reprint). Charles A. Hay and Henry E. Jacob (trans.). Minneapolis: Augsburg Publishing House, originally published in 1899.

Small, Dwight Hervey. *The Biblical Basis for Infant Baptism*. Westwood, N.J.: Fleming H. Revell, 1959.

Stoeckhardt, George. *Exegetical Lectures on the First Epistle of Paul to the Corinthians*. H. W. Degner (trans.). Fort Wayne: Concordia Theological Seminary, 1969.

Strong, James. *A Concise Dictionary of the Words of the Greek New Testament*. Nashville, TN: Abingdon, 1980.

Tappert, Theodore G. (trans. and ed.). *The Book of Concord*. Philadelphia: Fortress Press, 1959.

Thayer, Joseph Henry. *The New Thayer's Greek-English Lexicon of the New Testament*. Peabody, MA: Hendrickson Publishers, 1981.

Wall, William. *The History of Infant Baptism*. Vol. I. Oxford: Oxford University Press, 1844.

Whitaker, E. C. *Documents of the Baptismal Liturgy*. London: S.P.C.K., 1960, 1970.

Williams, Ronald J. *Hebrew Syntax: An Outline*. Second Ed. Toronto: University of Toronto Press, 1976.

ADDITIONAL BIBLIOGRAPHY:
Lingering Questions

Chrysostom, John. *Homily on the Epistle of Paul to the Corinthians*. Vol. 12 of *The Nicene and Post-Nicene Fathers,* Series 1. Philip Schaff and Henry Wace (eds.) Reprint. Peabody, MA: Hendrickson Publishers, 1994.

Jerome. *Letters and Select Works*. Vol. 6 of *The Nicene and Post-Nicene Fathers,* Series 2. Philip Schaff and Henry Wace (eds.) Reprint. Peabody, MA: Hendrickson Publishers, 1994.

Dale, James W. *Classic Baptism: An Inquiry into the Meaning of the Word as Determined by the Usage of Classical Greek Writers*. Reprint. Phillipsburg, NJ: Presbyterian and Reformed Publishing, 1989.

Dale, James W. *Judaic Baptism An Inquiry into the Meaning of the Word as Determined by the Usage of Classical Greek Writers*. Reprint. Phillipsburg, NJ: Presbyterian and Reformed Publishing, 1991.

Das, A. Andrew. "Acts 8: Water Baptism and the Spirit." *Concordia Journal* 19 (1993): 108-34.

Hull, Michael F. *Baptism on Account of the Dead (1 Cor 15:29): An Act of Faith in the Resurrection*. Academia Biblica 22. Atlanta: Society of Biblical Literature, 2005.

Hutchings, Samuel. *The Mode of Christian Baptism*. Boston: Congregational Publishing Society, 1874.

Kerr, James. *A Treatise on the Mode of Baptism*. Steubenville, OH: Abner L. Frazer, 1844.

McKnight, Scot. "The Warning Passages of Hebrews: A Formal Analysis and Theological Conclusions." *Trinity Journal* 13 (1992): 21-59.

Plutarch. *Moralia*. Frank Cole Babbitt et al. (trans.) 16 vols. Loeb Classical Library. Cambridge: Harvard University Press, 1927–2004.

Polybius. *Histories*. W. R. Paton (trans.) 8 vols. Loeb Classical Library. Cambridge: Harvard University Press, 1922–1927.

Rogers, Clement Francis. "Baptism and Christian Archaeology." Part 4 of Vol. 5 of *Studia Biblica et Ecclesiastica*. London: Oxford University Press, 1903: 239-357.

Schnackenburg, Rudolf. *The Gospel According to St. John*. 3 vols. New York: Seabury Press, 1980.

Strabo. *Geography*. Horace Leonard Jones (trans.) Loeb Classical Library. Cambridge: Harvard University Press, 1929.

Thiselton, Anthony C. *The First Epistle to the Corinthians*. The New International Greek Testament Commentary. Grand Rapids: William B. Eerdmans Publishing Company, 2000.

IMPACT
YOUR FAITH

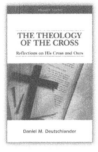
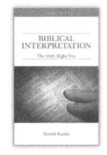
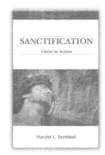

Develop a greater knowledge about essential topics of faith with the Impact Series. Each book shares relevant, practical, and meaningful truths and applications for you and all Christians today. Explore eye-opening questions about doctrine, culture, and more.

† The Theology of the Cross	† Law & Gospel
† The Narrow Lutheran Middle	† Baptized Into God's Family
† A Tale of Two Synods	† Sanctification
† Biblical Interpretation	† Gospel Motivation

God's Word works through these and other titles in the Impact Series to help you understand important issues and enrich your faith. **Subscribe today to save 25%!*** You will receive two books every two months in the order you choose until your collection is complete.

Call 800-662-6022 or visit www.nph.net/impact to see the current list of titles and to learn more.

*Future series offers will not exceed this 25% discount off the regular cover price. No further discounts apply. All orders are subject to shipping and handling fees and sales tax where applicable.

NORTHWESTERN PUBLISHING HOUSE

www.nph.net

NPH
EXTRA
PROGRAM

Find us on
Facebook